Management Techniques
for Solving
School Personnel Problems

OTHER BOOKS BY THE AUTHOR:

EDUCATOR'S DISCIPLINE HANDBOOK, Parker Publishing Company, Inc.,
West Nyack, New York

Management Techniques
for Solving
School Personnel Problems

Robert D. Ramsey, Ed. D.
Associate Superintendent of Schools
Independent School District No. 283
St. Louis Park, Minnesota

Parker Publishing Company, Inc.
West Nyack, New York

© 1984, *by*

PARKER PUBLISHING COMPANY, INC.

West Nyack, N.Y.

Third Printing . . . . . April 1988

Library of Congress Cataloging in Publication Data

Ramsey, Robert D.
  Management techniques for solving school personnel
problems.

  Bibliography: p. 187
  Includes index.
  1. School personnel management—United States.
I. Title.
LB2831.5R35   1984   371.2'01'0973   84-3146

ISBN 0-13-549841-4

Printed in the United States of America

To my beloved son and daughter, Jeff and Kim, who have been the recipients of my amateurish personnel management practices on the homefront for many years.

About the Author

Robert D. Ramsey is currently Associate Superintendent in St. Louis Park, Minnesota. His training includes B.S., M.S. and Ed. D. degrees from the University of Kansas, and his professional experience covers 25 years as a teacher, counselor, curriculum director, and administrator.

Dr. Ramsey is the author of the *Educator's Discipline Handbook* and has contributed numerous articles to leading educational journals.

About This Handbook

For the first time, this easy-to-read handbook provides both beginning and experienced administrators with a practical guide to promoting productivity and solving the most common personnel problems confronting today's schools. In straightforward, simple language, this handbook offers school-tested suggestions for dealing with such ongoing issues as motivating personnel, minimizing labor relations conflicts, bolstering staff morale, preventing burnout, improving weak teachers, and rejuvenating senior staff members. Key features include:

- Sixty-five Basic Personnel Skills for Administrators
- A Game Plan for Conducting Effective Negotiations
- Key Factors in Defusing Teacher Grievances
- How to Ease the Pain When Layoffs Come
- Essential Building Blocks for Better Morale
- Pointers for Paying Special Attention to Support Personnel
- Using a Job Target Approach to Staff Improvement
- Immediate Measures for Solving Teachers' Discipline Problems
- Fifty Ways to Make Every Teacher Better
- Action Steps in Improving Teacher–Parent Relations
- Practical Ways to Revitalize Veteran Teachers
- A Practical Design for Promoting Staff Wellness
- Twenty-five Remedies for Staff Stress
- Chapter-by-Chapter Appendices

In the rapidly changing context of today's schools, such a reference book has become a must for every modern administrator. Skills in personnel management have become the linchpin of leadership. The productivity of school personnel is being questioned increasingly by large segments of the public. At the same time, a new breed of professional has emerged in the school work force across the nation. Today's teachers demand more autonomy, greater participation in decision making, and bigger payoffs, while rejecting much of the responsibility for the nonteaching functions of education.

Bolstered by the power and success of the union movement, these teachers do not respond to traditional school personnel administration approaches. Thus, positive personnel management and the successful resolution of a growing array of staff problems are now top priorities for school administrators throughout the country. This handbook was developed especially to fill the need for a one-volume, practical guide to all of the essential information and know-how on personnel management for every educational leader today.

Of particular importance are two special chapters that spell out concrete, workable ways for handling every aspect of sensitive school labor relations issues— including the nuts and bolts of dealing with teacher strikes.

The handbook also provides real, nitty-gritty solutions to perplexing personnel problems such as absenteeism, alcoholism, and drug abuse. Other action-oriented sections of the guide include:

- Understanding the New Breed in the Educational Work Force
- Contract Perks That Perk Up Teachers
- Guidelines for Teachers' Political and Religious Activity
- Essentials for Easing Internal Staff Squabbles
- Ten Obstacles to Positive Staff Performance
- Practical Ways to Match Teaching and Learning Styles
- Elements of a Successful Strike Plan
- Sure-Fire Steps for Opening Up the System

Best of all, each chapter of the handbook contains a bonanza of specific examples, sample action plans, and understandable checklists that can be used to help any school staff become more effective and productive. The final chapter brings it all together by outlining a common-sense approach to positive personnel management through practical application of the encouraging process and the concept of "humanagement."

A special added feature of this unique guide is an unprecedented chapter-by-chapter supplement filled with suggestions and examples for putting positive personnel practices to work immediately in any situation. The chapter supplements assist readers in applying and implementing the many innovative aids described throughout the book.

Educators at all levels will find this guide an invaluable resource for solving today's common school staff problems. It serves as a comprehensive overview of modern school personnel practices. In addition, each separate chapter provides workable how-to hints on specific problems that can be referred to again and again. It is hoped that *Management Techniques for Solving School Personnel Problems* can fill a necessary niche in the professional library of each practicing educator who cares about the people he or she motivates and manages in the school setting.

Robert D. Ramsey, Ed. D.

Acknowledgments

It is impossible to recognize properly the many mentors, coworkers, and colleagues who have contributed to the concepts and developed the techniques presented in this guide.

However, I must acknowledge the tireless and talented efforts of Elaine Lerdall and my wife Joyce in the preparation of the manuscript. Without their able assistance, this work could not have been completed.

Contents

Contents

Management Techniques
for Solving
School Personnel Problems

1

How to Boost Productivity Through an Overall Program of Positive Personnel Management

A combination of dramatic changes and subtle shifts has transformed the public school from a relatively simple social system of clearcut roles and rules to a highly complex community of interdependent forces and relationships. The mushrooming of formalized labor relations, sweeping societal changes and expectations, rapid enrollment shifts, plummeting fiscal resources, and the evolution of a new breed in the work force all have contributed to reshaping today's school and the management of personnel in all school settings.

Against this backdrop of upheaval, traditional approaches to administering schools and school staffs have become dysfunctional. More than ever before, school leaders must be conscious of the relationship of productivity and cost-effectiveness to positive personnel management practices. Thus, educational executives at all levels are finding it necessary to learn new skills and techniques in personnel management.

Effective administration of the human resources in today's schools increasingly rests on the following six fundamental principles of personnel management, which have been recognized in the private sector for many years:

1. Leadership today is essentially a matter of building cooperation rather than commanding obedience.
2. How an organization, whether a private company or a public school, manages its human resources determines its productivity, its internal health as a work place, and its capacity to cope with crisis.

17

3. Individuals operate most efficiently and effectively when they feel sustained, valued, useful, and recognized.

4. Very few professionally trained people can continue to be effective over a long period of time if their work is perceived to be mostly mundane or negative in nature.

5. Managerial expectations are fundamental in fostering positive attitudes toward the institution and the institution's goals, which are essential to maximal productivity.

6. Vitality in any organization is increased when downward loyalty is evident and exercised.

The purpose of this handbook is to provide concrete, easy-to-understand ways for educational leaders to apply these principles in any school and to develop a well-rounded program of positive personnel management, which will reduce personnel problems and maximize productivity and effectiveness on the part of the total school staff.

UNDERSTANDING THE NEW BREED
IN THE EDUCATIONAL WORK FORCE

The first step in adopting a modern approach to managing human resources in schools is to understand fully the nature of the new work force that is rapidly occupying classrooms in most of the nation.

As in business and industry, many schools are finding that a growing number of employees espouse views and values that are radically different from those held by workers in the past. This new breed in the educational work force includes both the more militant young turks, fresh from teacher-training institutions, and mature staff members who feel they have earned their wings and have established themselves as veteran professionals. The new breed also can be found in increasing numbers among clerical and other classified employees.

Although some seasoned administrators are alarmed by the modern attitudes and actions of staff members, there is no evidence to suggest that the new breed is any less effective in the classroom than teachers in the past. In fact, many observers believe that the new breed of teacher is probably more successful in working with the new breed of students in today's schools.

The priorities and beliefs of the modern teacher are inherently no better or worse than those held by previous generations of educators—they are only different. The attitudes of today's teachers seem to reflect many of the changes that have occurred in society, appear to be shared by workers in almost all fields, and may constitute the work ethic of the future. It is essential, however, for administrators and other leaders to realize that changes in employee psychology require changes in leadership styles.

In order to adopt a management style that works with today's educational work force, administrators must, first of all, understand the concerns that lie at the heart of the employees' value system. Employee concerns must become management concerns if high morale and effective working relationships are to exist. In schools, as elsewhere, the human capital is ultimately the real catalyst for productivity.

Three primary characteristics differentiate present employees from traditional building staff: (1) a refusal to acquiesce to administrative paternalism, (2) a growing interest in self-representation at the bargaining table, and (3) an unwillingness to accept any condescending attitudes on the part of administrators about their school or their teachers.

In addition to these characteristics, modern school managers deal increasingly with employees who:

- Don't fear superiors (want to work on a first name basis with the boss).
- Ask "why" questions and expect answers.
- Expect to be consulted and to have influence.
- Value opportunity, personal freedom, satisfaction, organizational recognition, and freedom to seek new and better ways of doing things.
- Feel entitled to register complaints, to have privacy, and to receive assignments that rise above routine and provide opportunities for growth.
- Are better educated and more assertive than equivalent personnel in the past.
- Expect work that is relevant, purposeful, and appreciated.
- Tend to value play as much as work.
- Resent being treated as subordinates.
- Tend to use sick leave and other benefits extensively.
- Reflect lower loyalty to organizational goals, priorities, and commitments.
- Value vacations and other benefit provisions.
- Are not reticent about criticizing the system and its leadership.
- Often stand on the edge of alienation from the institution.
- Do not rely on their job as the sole source of self-esteem.

SIXTY-FIVE BASIC PERSONNEL SKILLS FOR ADMINISTRATORS

Based on the profile of the new breed of educational employee outlined above, administrators must develop nontraditional strategies for shaping a productive staff team and utilizing the human resources of the school effectively.

In the modern milieu of school personnel administration, many traditional practices simply don't work. Little progress can be expected in increasing productivity, goal attainment, or organizational unity if management's only solutions are lectures aimed at getting teachers to work harder or official edicts admonishing staff members to work together efficiently and effectively.

Changing times and the new breed in the educational work force demand a new view of leadership as positive action, not mere position. The following are 65 specific skills that expanding numbers of successful administrators are finding to be crucial for effective personnel management in today's school setting:

1. Capacity to release the abilities of others
2. Ability to set priorities (for self and others) and to direct energies toward important tasks
3. Listening skills
4. Capacity to understand and manage change
5. Openness to experience
6. A sixth sense in anticipating complaints or problems
7. Consensus-building skills
8. Ability to manage disappointment
9. A tolerance for turbulence
10. Capability of activating and directing human resources
11. Observation skills
12. Ability to set realistic goals for self and others
13. A proactive, positive approach to problems
14. A relaxed manner in dealing with people
15. Conferencing skills
16. Capacity to blend confidence and healthy doubt
17. Ability to manage oneself in order to manage others (successful leaders are in touch with themselves)
18. Awareness of employee values
19. Skill in removing human or psychological barriers
20. Courage to be imperfect
21. Ability to heighten motivation
22. Supporting skills
23. Capacity to convey high expectations of success
24. Skills in expediting and facilitating
25. Ability to help others operate at maximum efficiency and effectiveness
26. Communication skills
27. Capability of integrating an emphasis on a high-tech, high-touch learning and working environment
28. Diplomacy
29. Ability to maximize cooperation
30. Risk-taking skills
31. Capability of self-disclosure
32. An open posture

33. A person-oriented approach to problem solving
34. Venturesomeness
35. Ability to elicit and enhance loyalty
36. Negotiating skills
37. Authenticity
38. Capacity to value and encourage growth
39. Process skills
40. Optimism
41. Ability to refuse to have all the answers
42. Skills in relational leadership (ability to stress relationships and linkages)
43. Ability to delegate coupled with an understanding that some administrative reponsibilities are unsharable (see Figure 1–1, Mini-Checklist for Delegating Authority)
44. Counseling skills
45. Capacity to avoid spinning wheels over trifles such as communication gaps, power struggles, personality conflicts, politics, petty bickering, and so on
46. Problem-solving skills
47. Acceptance of employees as coworkers
48. Ability to work in groups
49. Skills in organizational development (participatory decision making)
50. A human resource orientation (many districts are now expanding the traditional view of the position of personnel director to include responsibility for total human resource management and staff development—see Figure 1–2, Sample Position Description)
51. Brokering skills
52. Ability to create a climate for realizing the potential of each individual involved
53. Capacity to clarify role expectations
54. Skills in eclectic (situational) leadership
55. Face-to-face skills
56. Conflict management skills (capacity to use conflict to promote growth)
57. Nonverbal communication skills, which often convey suggestions, authenticity, and feelings more efficiently and accurately than verbal communication skills
58. Learning skills
59. Ability to accept and enhance differences among individuals and groups
60. Capacity to understand and work with hidden agendas
61. Skills in dealing with interpersonal confrontation

MINI-CHECKLIST FOR DELEGATING AUTHORITY

☑ Define task and expected results.

☑ Allow party to whom authority is delegated to determine methods of accomplishment.

☑ Inform others of delegated authority.

☑ Get out of the way.

☑ Provide feedback when task is completed.

☑ Do not take the task back once it has been delegated.

Figure 1–1

DIRECTOR OF HUMAN RESOURCES AND STAFF DEVELOPMENT
(Sample Position Description)

<u>Responsibilities:</u>

● Take overall responsibility for districtwide personnel administration functions for certified and classified staff.

● Work with principals and directors in selection, assignment, transfer, and evaluation of personnel.

● Establish processes and monitor their results to ensure compliance with all personnel aspects of federal and state guidelines.

● Design, implement, and evaluate an ongoing program of staff development addressing the current and emerging needs of the district.

● Monitor and evaluate the district's staff wellness program.

● Direct the staff negotiation process.

● Manage the issuance of contracts, the development and maintenance of personnel records, and the preparation of required reports and budget information.

● Assist principals and staffs in the design and implementation of staff development programs that have been identified as needs in their unique situation.

● Work with business office personnel in coordinating records and information affecting payroll and risk management.

Figure 1–2

62. Team-building skills
63. Capacity to be helpful and to avoid opportunism, exploitation, or manipulation
64. Skills in emphasizing the human basis for learning
65. Ability to arrange conditions and methods of operation so that people can achieve their own goals best by directing their efforts toward the realization of organizational objectives

TWO DOZEN DO'S AND DON'TS OF MODERN PERSONNEL MANAGEMENT

In addition to the leadership skills enumerated above, the rudiments of successful school staff supervision are reflected in the following widely accepted standards of modern personnel management:

Do	*Don't*
Inform staff of goals.	Feel superior.
Exhibit consistent behavior.	Rely on telling.
Evaluate performance fairly.	Fear mistakes.
Believe employees want to succeed.	Feel threatened or intimidated.
Be helpful and hospitable.	Impose decisions.
Tolerate ambiguity.	Pontificate.
Praise, be genuinely pleased with the successes of coworkers.	Accentuate negatives.
Recognize the contributions of all staff members.	Change too much too fast.
Build on strengths.	Reinforce a caste system in the school.
Stress collaborative, collegial problem solving.	Play games with collective bargaining.
Understand and use the concept of alternative futures that can be shaped by today's decisions and actions.	Be phony.
	Bemoan the loss of the good old professional teachers of yesteryear.

ACTION STEPS IN ANGER MANAGEMENT FOR ADMINISTRATORS

One further essential element for successfully orchestrating relationships and managing the human resources in the school is the ability of the administrator to keep cool and to avoid taking actions in anger.

The best laid plans for positive personnel management can sometimes be disrupted or destroyed when school leaders become frustrated and act in anger. Obviously, the pressures of mounting teacher militancy, escalating parental expectations, and emotion-laden labor relations sometimes make it tempting for officials to succumb to anger and to strike out at perceived adversaries. Nevertheless, the essence of harmonious relationships within any school rests on a leader who models calm confidence and a reasoned approach to problem solving. When actions are dictated by anger, positive results seldom ensue.

To achieve the level of equanimity required for effective handling of the human affairs of the school, some administrators have found the following seven steps in anger management to be valuable tools:

1. Know what makes you angry.
2. Know the symptoms of anger.
3. Know your tolerance levels.
4. Avoid anger-provoking situations where possible.
5. If at all possible, express frankly what's bothering you, *preferably* to the source of the anger.
6. Do something physical and constructive to dissipate angry feelings (for example, painting, gardening, jogging, and so on).
7. When necessary, act out anger in harmless ways (such as punching pillows, writing a vehement letter and then destroying it, breaking something unimportant, buying a voodoo doll).

The introductory information in this chapter lays the foundation for building a program of positive personnel management in the school setting. The remainder of the handbook provides detailed analyses of each of the key components necessary to maintain high morale, to maximize productivity, to generate effective teamwork, and to ensure healthy working relationships in schools at any level.

CHAPTER SUPPLEMENTS

The following chapter supplements are included to illustrate the principles outlined in this chapter.

Contents:

- A Prototype Program for Promoting Productivity Through Professional Growth
- Job-Related Questions for Interviewing Teachers
- Sample Hiring and Promotion Report

A PROTOTYPE PROGRAM FOR
PROMOTING PRODUCTIVITY
THROUGH PROFESSIONAL GROWTH

One way to enhance productivity is through in-service training, which provides immediate tools for more effective teamwork as well as follow-up exposures that serve as reminders and reinforcers. Variations on the following two-pronged program can be adapted to any school setting, regardless of size.

1. Initial In-service

- <u>Topic and Organization</u>—A voluntary, two-hour workshop on team building.

- <u>Purpose</u>—To heighten overall productivity by presenting strategies with which a total school staff community can learn to interact and work together cooperatively in an atmosphere of mutual respect.

- <u>Topics</u>—Cooperative interaction with colleagues
  Developing support for one another
  Resolving on-the-job conflicts

2. Follow-up Model

- <u>Medium</u>*—Series of weekly motivational attitude-building posters designed to follow up on the initial in-service with reinforcement messages that can speak to individual employees in a nonthreatening manner.

- <u>Messages</u>—Understanding institutional goals
  Achieving individual interests through group goals
  Excessive absenteeism
  Negative attitudes
  Respect for cooperation and teamwork
  Principles of good job performance
  Individual contributions count

---

*A commercial program package of such "Persuasive Posters" is available from Smith Associates, Asbury Avenue, Farmingdale, New Jersey 07727.

JOB-RELATED QUESTIONS FOR
INTERVIEWING TEACHERS

Changing times and a new breed of candidates for teaching positions require a different focus in staff selection. Traditional inquiries limited to college courses taken and extracurricular interests are not sufficient to identify teachers who are capable of promoting productivity in their own classrooms and throughout the entire school. Interviewers today are well advised to concentrate on what candidates have done rather than promises of what will be done. These sample interview questions point up the areas of emphasis and the objective criteria needed to assemble an effective school staff in the 1980s.

1. How would you describe your teaching style? What evidence or indicators lead you to this conclusion?

2. Of what accomplishment in your professional career are you most proud?

3. What was the most difficult teaching assignment or task you ever had to undertake?

4. What do you see as your most critical role and function as an instructional leader in the classroom?

5. What kind of working relationship do you envision among teachers? Between teachers and administration?

6. If you had to highlight your personal philosophy of education in a few sentences, what would you include?

7. How would you describe the roles of basics and of balance in a modern school program?

8. What are your long-range professional goals and interests in education?

9. What is your concept of a modern elementary (or secondary) school? What changes do you foresee in the next century?

10. How would you proceed to get parent support, cooperation, and involvement in your instructional program?

11. What kind of feedback would you provide for students, parents, and administration?

12. What is your process for dealing with student and parent concerns?

13. If you could rid yourself of some of your most nonproductive responsibilities, what would they be?

14. How would you create a climate of openness in your classroom?

15. What role should pupils play in determining or influencing instructional decisions?

16. How do you achieve appropriate discipline in the classroom?

17. What personal qualities do you possess that enhance your teaching effectiveness?

18. What do you see as the role of the teacher in curriculum development?

19. What level of concern do you have for the affective side of education?

**JOB-RELATED QUESTIONS FOR
INTERVIEWING TEACHERS (continued)**

20. What do you foresee as the role of technology in education during the next decade?

21. How do you motivate students toward necessary improvement?

22. How do you encourage and utilize volunteers in the classroom?

23. What kinds of school–home activities do you carry on?

24. What is your view of the place of controversial issues or speakers in the classroom?

25. What is the importance of teamwork in the operation of a school?

26. What understanding do you have of the differences in individual learning styles? How do you use this information in the classroom?

27. What is your definition of computer or technological literacy? How important is this literacy for teachers? To what extent are you computer-literate?

28. How would you evaluate the effectiveness of your instructional program and personal performance?

29. Do you believe in faculty advisory councils? Why or why not?

30. How would you use the results of your performance evaluation?

31. What personal steps will you take to facilitate your own ongoing professional and self-development?

32. How can management help you to live up to your expectations?

SAMPLE HIRING AND PROMOTION REPORT

During a period of social sensitivity regarding fair employment practices, equal opportunity, affirmative action, and antidiscrimination, it is essential for school leaders to monitor and document all personnel procedures involving hiring and promotion as well as dismissal or placement on unrequested leave. The following sample report form can assist administrators in keeping a handle on staffing practices and maintaining adequate records in case of possible grievance action or litigation.

Date _____

Filed by _____

1. Position filled _____

2. New employee is (circle appropriate responses)

certified staff	female	Caucasian	Asian	Hispanic surname

noncertified staff	male	Black	Native American

3. How and where position advertised _____

	F	M	Cauc.	Black	Asian	NA	SN
4. Number of persons in same department or job category							
5. Number of applicants (total)							
6. Number of applicants interviewed							

7. Was an interviewing committee used? Yes _____ No _____

2

Secrets of Successful School Labor Relations

Formalized collective bargaining is rapidly becoming the norm as the prevailing framework for board–administration–staff relations in public schools throughout the nation. Thus, conducting successful and productive labor relations is increasingly the focal point for positive personnel management in schools.

The swift transition from traditional relationships to tightly defined procedures and processes governed by a negotiated agreement has caught many school officials off-guard. Because collective bargaining is a relatively new experience for many educators and because there are a number of fundamental differences between labor relations in the public and private sectors, school leaders are being called on to learn an entirely new set of skills, roles, and rules of conduct.

Many administrators have viewed the advent of formal labor relations in the public schools with alarm, foretelling the demise of sound instruction, participatory decision making, and positive staff relationships. Obviously, experience across the country has not proved these doomsday forecasts to be accurate.

Collective bargaining is, by nature, an adversarial situation, but it can also be managed in ways that produce positive outcomes.

Since every facet of the educational enterprise is touched by the growth of collective bargaining rights for virtually all categories of employees, it is imperative that administrators and other leaders understand the process and acquire the necessary skills to function effectively within a labor relations structure. The following sections of this chapter identify the essentials for maintaining successful labor relations in every school setting.

A GAME PLAN FOR CONDUCTING EFFECTIVE NEGOTIATIONS

Developing a manageable negotiations process that results in a workable and livable master agreement is basic to sound labor relations in any school or school system. Achieving this goal is complicated, however, by the unique features that characterize collective bargaining in a public institution as opposed to a private business or industry (for example, public sector managers do not have the immediate profit-and-loss incentives to resist union demands that exist in the corporate or business world). In any educational setting, the parties responsible for conducting negotiations must not only be concerned with protecting the right of the governing body to govern and the right of management to manage, but they also must consider the best interests of students, parents, employees, and the public at large.

In most school situations, collective bargaining is a *developmental* process. Initially, the emphasis is on assuming adversarial positions and focusing almost exclusively on money issues (despite the fact that many studies show that collective bargaining is not the primary factor in determining the level of compensation and may, in fact, have a negative impact resulting in the only real rewards going to union leaders, negotiators, and so on).

With experience over time, however, most school districts evolve a more sophisticated system of relationships, which reflects mutual concerns, mutual respect, and joint efforts to solve mutual problems, as depicted in Figure 2–1.

Throughout this maturing process, it is necessary for all managers to recognize that the ongoing relationships within the school community are more important than the immediate outcomes of any single cycle of negotiations.

Within the context of school collective bargaining described above, the following table-tested tips have assisted countless administrators in conducting effective negotiations aimed at promoting long-term, positive personnel management:

- Select a chief negotiator with extreme care (this may be the most important decision in the total negotiations process). This person may be

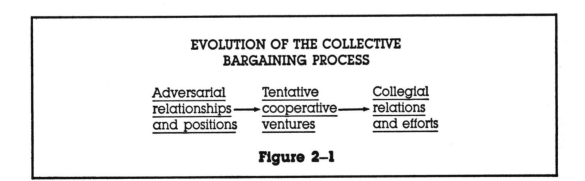

**EVOLUTION OF THE COLLECTIVE
BARGAINING PROCESS**

Adversarial ⟶ Tentative ⟶ Collegial
relationships   cooperative   relations
and positions   ventures   and efforts

Figure 2–1

chosen from existing staff; however, where experience is limited, it is often advantageous to hire a competent outside consultant. In any case, the chief spokesperson should be knowledgeable, experienced, and articulate.

- Identify the remainder of the negotiating team with equal caution. The entire team must reflect a balance of expertise and, above all, must represent a compatible unit that can function effectively under pressure. (Many districts have found it to be disadvantageous to include board members or the superintendent in the group that represents the district directly at the table during each bargaining session.)

- Do your homework carefully and completely. A thorough review of the existing contract based on input from the entire administrative team (including principals) should be conducted before the initial negotiating session. Special attention should be devoted to problem areas, language difficulties, ambiguities, inconsistencies, experience with grievances, and the outcomes of any arbitration awards related to the agreement.

- Know the law (and relevant court decisions) pertinent to public school collective bargaining in the particular state involved.

- Know the existing contract forward and backward. (Some administrators involved in negotiations have found it helpful to keep a separate file on each article of the agreement.)

- Recognize that listening is one of the chief tools of the successful negotiator. It is essential for everyone participating in collective bargaining, to hear what the other side is saying and to attempt to perceive the subtleties and implications involved. Sometimes, convincing the other side that their case has been heard is as important as the final product of the negotiating process.

- Develop a defensible management position for each proposal forwarded by the teachers' bargaining unit.

- Keep all key parties (board, superintendent, principals, and so on) fully informed of the status and progress of negotiations at all times. The teachers' unit probably will issue a periodic newsletter to keep members up to date throughout the bargaining process. It is often advisable for the district to do likewise.

- Focus on problems and possible solutions rather than stated positions.

- Be willing to provide the opposing party with all legitimate information that is part of the public records—don't play games.

- Be cooperative in scheduling bargaining sessions at reasonable times and places.

- Emphasize the importance of concluding negotiations within the legal limits for budget adoption.

- Recognize that there are seldom clear winners or losers at the bargaining table.
- Appreciate the public's interest in the bargaining process and its outcome, but attempt to avoid conducting negotiations in a fishbowl. (In some states, open meeting laws unduly hamper timely and productive collective bargaining and do a disservice to the public.)
- Be patient—negotiations can become an agonizingly protracted process, and all parties should be prepared to let things run their course.
- Enter every bargaining session with the belief that both parties sincerely desire an agreement.
- Operate in good faith at all times during collective bargaining.
- Remain firm in defining what items and areas are negotiable.
- Don't assume anything during negotiations.
- Appreciate the other party's need for some theatrics and posturing. All collective bargaining contains an element of ritual.
- Recognize a smokescreen when you see one.
- Offer counterproposals wherever appropriate.
- Generate new options when an impasse appears imminent.
- Don't make promises you can't keep. The chief negotiator should never exceed his or her authority.
- Don't take personally pointed remarks made at the table.
- Recognize that each side must win something in order to establish their legitimacy and to be in a position to sell the final agreement to their constituency.
- Don't be afraid of fact finding, mediation, or arbitration as an ultimate solution to difficult negotiations.
- Recognize that contract language is all-important. The final written agreement constitutes the rules for relationships between both parties for the duration of the contract. Don't rush the approval of specific language. It is always easier to modify language before it is incorporated into a ratified agreement than it is to change it later.
- Be aware that the final, important decisions often are reached when there are only two people in the room.

OUTLINE FOR A WORKABLE MASTER CONTRACT

When all of the furor of a lively negotiation process subsides, the only tangible outcome is a master agreement that will govern much of the affairs of the school for a substantial period of time.

As stated earlier, it is usually the nature of the bargaining process and the ongoing relationships that determine the soundness of labor relations and personnel management in the school. Nevertheless, it is difficult to overstate the importance of each and every negotiated agreement.

A good contract can ease or avoid a multitude of sticky situations and provide a framework for productive working relationships. A bad contract can cause constant confusion, frustration, ill will, and disharmony among the ranks of employees at any level.

Many seasoned negotiators describe a good contract as being "lean and mean." This simply implies a clear agreement that is concise and comprehensible while addressing the majority of negotiable issues existing in the school.

Although there is no accepted universal format or outline for master agreements in schools, the model in Figure 2–2 (page 37) represents the most common elements found in effective contracts from many districts.

SAMPLE CONTRACT PROVISIONS THAT WORK

The master agreement serves as a guide for much of the labor or personnel relations in the school and as a tool that can be used by all parties involved to avoid or resolve problems of many kinds. The success of any contract rests on both the content and the language. An effective contract says exactly what the bargaining parties agreed and intended to say in a way that is understandable to all parties covered by the agreement.

SAMPLE PROVISIONS FROM TEACHER CONTRACTS

Figures 2–3A through 2–6C contain samples of working contract provisions that reflect precise content statements expressed in precise contract language. The examples provided have been selected from actual agreements relating to several categories of employee groups within the school. (See pages 38–44.)

CONTRACT PERKS THAT PERK UP TEACHERS

One way that school managers can utilize the collective bargaining process as a tool for fostering improved morale, productivity, and harmonious relationships is to permit inclusion of certain popular "perks" in contracts for teachers or other personnel. Often, these minor concessions or additional benefits entail minimal costs and result in substantial payoffs in terms of good will and a feeling by the staff that the school is a human-oriented setting in which to work and teach.

Below are 11 possible benefit provisions, that can perk up staff relations and the overall school climate, which have been included in some contracts around the country:

1. Selection by employees from a "cafeteria" of benefits within certain dollar amount limits (for example, some employees may need child care assistance but not health insurance).

2. Paid health insurance that covers costs of treatment for chemical dependency and other drug-related problems.

3. Child care leave provisions.

4. Short-term leaves (sabbatical leaves, general leaves of absence, and so on) of one quarter or one semester duration.

5. One or two days of annual personal leave (no reason required).

6. Salary credit for in-service courses, workshops, courses by outside agencies other than colleges or universities (see Figure 2–7, page 45).

7. Payroll deductions for United Way, professional dues, and credit union loans or savings deposits.

8. Provisions for shared-time positions (such as tandem teaching) with full or partial fringe benefits.

9. Payment of professional dues for principals and other administrators.

10. Limited matching district funds for employee tax-sheltered annuities.

11. Early retirement incentives.

KEY FACTORS IN DEFUSING TEACHER GRIEVANCES

No matter how carefully designed and developed, contracts will always remain imperfect instruments that lend themselves to varied interpretations and are administered by fallible human beings who can make mistakes. Thus, some provision for a systematic grievance procedure (a process for resolving disagreements over contract interpretation and application) is essential in every master agreement. How often this procedure is used may be one way to evaluate the effectiveness of the contract.

A workable grievance procedure should be easy to understand and simple to use. An example of one such grievance provision appears in Figure 2–8 on page 46.

Many school leaders have found that skill in administering the contract and in handling grievances is as important as the skills required in negotiating the agreement in the first place.

Sloppy, half-hearted, or insensitive processing of legitimate grievances can undermine months of effort to arrive at a just and workable contract and to establish a positive working climate for employees at all levels.

The following guidelines can assist practicing administrators in both large and small districts in dealing with difficult grievance situations in a professional manner and without jeopardizing other efforts to implement positive personnel practices.

- Make every effort to ensure that all parties understand what constitutes a grievable issue. It should be defined clearly in the contract that the formal grievance procedure is reserved for alleged violations of the written contract, not for every petty complaint, personality conflict, or personal problem an employee may experience.
- Follow the established grievance procedures (hearings, time lines, and so on) willingly and to the letter.
- Know the contract provisions thoroughly.
- Exert extra effort to resolve grievances informally whenever possible.
- Don't treat any formal grievance lightly or consider it frivolous.
- Listen to all parties involved.
- Assemble all pertinent facts diligently.
- Don't ridicule any grievance or grievant.
- Avoid stalling, deferring, or passing the buck.
- Never use guesswork in attempting to resolve a grievance. Rely on facts.
- Don't divert energy and attention toward extraneous issues.
- Retain your poise and humor, and refrain from losing your temper.
- Avoid implying any kind of threat at any point in the grievance process.
- Be professional, and don't take derogatory comments or allegations personally.
- Be direct in all questioning and in responding to any formal grievance.
- Have the courage to make unpopular decisions when necessary.
- Stick with your decisions.

The purpose of this chapter has been to dispel the commonly held concept that the advent of unionization and formal negotiations rings the death knell for positive personnel relations in schools.

The variety of suggestions provided above can help every school official to function effectively within the labyrinth of current labor relations and to use the tools of collective bargaining to enhance working conditions, morale, productivity, teamwork, school climate, and positive staff relations.

SUGGESTED CONTRACT FORMAT

1. Preamble—Purpose of the Agreement
2. Definitions of Terms
3. Recognition of Exclusive Bargaining Representative
4. School District (Management) Rights
5. Association (Union) Rights
6. School Year
7. School Day
8. Basic Compensation (Salary Schedule)
9. Extra Compensation
10. Group Insurance
11. Leave Provisions
12. Vacancies and Transfers
13. Unrequested Leave and Seniority Policy
14. Severance Pay and Early Retirement Provisions
15. Performance Appraisal (Evaluation)
16. Grievance Procedure
17. Labor–Management Committees
18. Miscellaneous Provisions
19. Duration of the Agreement
20. Appropriate Appendices and Attachments

Figure 2–2

DEFINITIONS OF TERMS

Section 1. School District—For purposes of this Agreement, the term "school district" shall mean the _____ school district, its school board, or designated representative(s) of the school board.

Section 2. Association—For purposes of this Agreement, the term "association" shall mean the _____ Association of Teachers or its designated representative(s).

Section 3. PELRA—For purposes of this Agreement, the term "PELRA" shall mean the Public Employment Labor Relations Act of 1971, as amended.

Section 4. Terms and Conditions of Employment— "Terms and conditions of employment" means the hours of employment, the compensation therefor (including fringe benefits except retirement contributions or benefits), and the employer's personnel policies affecting the working conditions of the employees. In the case of professional employees, the term does not mean educational policies of a school district. The terms in both cases are subject to the provisions of Section 179.66 regarding the rights of public employers and the scope of negotiations.

Section 5. Other Terms—Terms not defined in this Agreement shall have those meanings as defined by law.

Figure 2–3A

SCHOOL DISTRICT RIGHTS

Section 1. Inherent Managerial Rights—The parties recognize that the school board is not required to meet and negotiate on matters of inherent managerial policy, which include but are not limited to such areas of discretion or policy as the functions and programs of the employer, its overall budget, utilization of technology, the organizational structure, and selection, direction, and number of personnel, and that all management rights and management functions not expressly delegated in this Agreement are reserved to the school board. This section shall not be construed to limit the right of the association to meet and confer with the school district, pursuant to PELRA, regarding policies and matters not included under terms and conditions of employment.

Section 2. Management Responsibilities—The parties recognize the right and obligation of the school board to manage and conduct efficiently the operation of the school district within its legal limitations and with its primary obligation to provide educational opportunity for the students of the school district.

Section 3. Effect of Laws, Rules, and Regulations—The parties recognize that all teachers covered by this Agreement shall perform the teaching and reasonable teaching-related services prescribed by the school district. The parties also recognize the right, obligation, and duty of the school board and its duly designated officials to promulgate reasonable rules, regulations, directives, and orders from time to time as deemed necessary insofar as such reasonable rules, regulations, directives, and orders are not inconsistent with the terms of this Agreement. The parties further recognize that the school district, all teachers covered by this Agreement, and all provisions of this Agreement are subject to the laws of the State of _____, federal laws, rules and regulations of the State Board of Education, and valid rules, regulations, and orders of state and federal governmental agencies.

Figure 2–3B

UNREQUESTED LEAVE OF ABSENCE
AND SENIORITY POLICY

Section 1. Unrequested Leave—Both parties acknowledge that they are governed by applicable state statutes regarding unrequested leave of absence.

Section 2. Ties in Seniority—In the event of a staff reduction action affecting teachers whose first date of employment commenced on the same date and who have equal seniority, the selection of the teacher for purposes of discontinuance shall be at the discretion of the school district based upon criteria including performance, training, experience, skills in special assignments, and other relevant factors.

Section 3. Seniority List—The school district shall promulgate a seniority list of all teachers in the district. A teacher who disputes his or her standing in the list promulgated by the school district may process a grievance pursuant to the grievance procedure.

Section 4. Substitute from Recall List—A teacher on the recall list who is offered and accepts a substitute position shall be granted reinstatement rights for a period as provided by statute.

Figure 2–3C

SAMPLE PROVISIONS FROM CLERICAL
OR SECRETARIAL CONTRACTS

RECOGNITION OF EXCLUSIVE REPRESENTATIVE

Section 1. Recognition—The school board recognizes the _____ Association of Clerical Employees as the exclusive representative of clerical personnel employed by the school board of Independent School District No. XXX, which exclusive representative shall have those rights and duties as prescribed by law and as described in the provisions of this Agreement.

Section 2. Appropriate Unit—The exclusive representative shall represent all clerical personnel of the school district, including secretaries, paraprofessionals, clerks, teachers' aides, health aides, and hall monitors who are employed for more than 14 hours per week and for more than 100 work days per year, including those on leave of absence who are guaranteed a position upon their return, excluding secretaries to the superintendent, assistant superintendent, director of business affairs, employees in the personnel and administrative services offices, payroll clerk, and any other supervisory, confidential, and emergency employees. Also excluded are temporary or substitute clerical employees.

Figure 2–4A

PROBATIONARY PERIOD, SUSPENSION, AND DISCIPLINE DISCHARGE

Section 1. <u>Probationary Period</u>—An employee under the provisions of this Agreement shall serve a probationary period of six months of continuous service in the school district during which time the school district shall have the unqualified right to suspend without pay, discharge, or otherwise discipline such employee; and during this probationary period, the employee shall have no recourse to the grievance procedure insofar as suspension, discharge, or other discipline is concerned.

Section 2. <u>Suspension or Discharge</u>—An employee who has completed the probationary period may be suspended without pay, discharged, or disciplined only for just cause. An employee who has completed the probationary period and is suspended without pay, discharged, or otherwise disciplined shall have access to the grievance procedure.

Section 3. <u>Probationary Period, Change of Classification</u>—In addition to the initial probationary period, an employee transferred or promoted to a different classification shall serve a new probationary period of 60 calendar days in any such new classification. During this 60-day probationary period, if it is determined by the school district that the employee's performance in the new classification is unsatisfactory, the school district shall have the right to reassign the employee to his or her former classification.

Figure 2–4B

EVALUATION

Section 1. All formal evaluations of clerical personnel shall be conducted openly and with full knowledge of the employee concerned by an administrator or supervisor of the school district.

Section 2. All formal evaluations of clerical personnel shall be in writing. Two copies of the written evaluation shall be submitted to the employee at the time of the personal conference or within five working days thereafter, one to be signed and returned to the administration, the other to be retained by the employee. In the event that the employee feels that the evaluation was incomplete or unjust, the employee may put those objections in writing and have them attached to the evaluation report to be placed in the employee's personnel file. All evaluations shall be based on valid criteria.

Figure 2–4C

SAMPLE PROVISIONS FROM PRINCIPAL'S CONTRACTS

Section 6. Information—The parties agree that the association shall have access, upon reasonable notice, to appropriate and available information, not deemed confidential, necessary for the association to exercise its responsibilities as exclusive representative.

Figure 2–5A

Section 3. Request for Dues Checkoff—Principals shall have the right to dues checkoff for the association, provided that dues checkoff and the proceeds thereof shall not be allowed any principal organization that has lost its right to dues checkoff pursuant to state statute. Upon receipt of a properly executed authorization card of the principal involved, the school district shall deduct from the principal's paycheck the dues that the principal has agreed to pay to the principal organization during the period provided in said authorization. These deductions may be terminated by the principal by giving 30 days written notice to the school district business office to stop deductions. Deduction shall be made over 12 pay periods and transmitted to the association. The school district shall furnish monthly to the association an alphabetized list of its members from whom such deductions have been made.

Figure 2–5B

Section 8. Private and Personal Life—The private and personal life of a principal is not within the appropriate concern of the school district, providing such private and personal life does not adversely affect the principal's performance or ability to perform.

Figure 2–5C

SAMPLE PROVISIONS FROM DISTRICT ADMINISTRATOR'S CONTRACT

Physical Examination—Each administrator shall have a comprehensive physical examination every three years unless otherwise requested by the school board, the cost of which shall be borne by the school district. A report of the results of such examination shall be provided to the school district for inclusion in the administrator's personnel file.

Figure 2–6A

Professional Growth Week—Each administrator is entitled to use up to five days per year with pay for personal professional growth activities. These activities can include writing, speaking, consulting, teaching, and so on. Each administrator will submit an annual report to the superintendent on his or her utilization of these days. The superintendent will be notified of the administrator's intent to use one or more of the days before the time he or she intends to take them.

Figure 2–6B

Supplemental Health Care Expense Allowance—The school district shall allocate the sum of $750 per annum as a supplemental medical and dental expense fund to pay health-related expenses incurred by the administrator of his or her dependents that are not covered by the district's regular health insurance program. Such expenses shall include but not be limited to the following: doctor bills, dental bills, prescriptions, eye care, eyeglasses, and other health-related costs. Unused portions of the annual allowance may be carried over into the next year, but the total allowance shall not exceed $1500 in any one year. Upon cessation of employment, any unused balance in this account shall accrue to the school district and not to the individual.

Figure 2–6C

Section 6. Professional Growth Credits

1. Teachers who complete an approved in-service course shall be eligible for credit on the salary schedule on the basis of one quarter hour for each ten hours of class time.

2. Teachers also shall be granted salary schedule credit, on the basis of one quarter hour for each ten hours of participation, for successful completion of approved courses sponsored by outside agencies that meet the following criteria:

    a. No academic credit is granted.

    b. The experience must be in a field related to the teaching assignment.

    c. Participation occurs outside the regular school day.

    d. The participant's expenses are not paid by the school district.

3. Salary schedule credits, earned through any means described in this section, shall be limited to six quarter hours toward each block of fifteen quarter hours required for a lane change. A maximum of eighteen professional growth credits shall be considered for application on the salary schedule.

Figure 2–7

SAMPLE GRIEVANCE PROCEDURE

Section 1. Purpose and Procedures

   1. Good morale is maintained whenever problems arise by the sincere efforts of all persons concerned, working toward constructive solutions in an atmosphere of courtesy, cooperation, and good faith. The parties acknowledge that it is desirable for a staff member and his or her principal or supervisor to resolve grievances informally. However, since all matters cannot be resolved satisfactorily in this manner, a formal process must be provided as an alternative. This formal grievance procedure has been developed as a means of securing, at the lowest possible administrative level, prompt and equitable solutions to those disputes not settled on an informal basis.

   2. The parties agree that grievance proceedings shall be kept as informal and confidential as may be appropriate to any level of the procedure. Further, it is agreed that the investigation and processing of any grievance shall be conducted in a professional manner at such times as not to cause undue interruptions of established teaching schedules.

Section 2. Representatives—The school district may be represented during any step of this procedure by its designated representative. The teacher may be represented during any step of this procedure by the association. In the event that a teacher does not desire representation by the association or the association does not process the grievance, the association shall not assume any responsibility, including the cost, for the grievance. However, in such case, the individual grievant(s) shall be responsible for the appropriate share of expenses.

Section 3. Grievance Definition—A "grievance" shall mean an allegation by a teacher or a group of teachers resulting from a dispute or disagreement regarding the interpretation or application of any term or terms of the agreement.

Section 4. Adjustment of Grievance—The parties shall attempt to adjust all grievances that may arise during the course of employment of any teacher within the school district in the following manner. If a teacher believes there has been a grievance, he or she shall discuss the matter with the responsible administrator in an attempt to arrive at a satisfactory solution. If the grievance is not resolved as a result of this meeting, the grievance shall be reduced to writing, setting forth the facts and the specific provisions of the Agreement allegedly violated and the particular relief sought. An alleged grievance must be presented in writing as promptly as possible and within 20 days of the occurrence of the act or within 20 days after the teacher acquired or, through the use of responsible diligence, should have acquired knowledge of the alleged violation. Failure to file a grievance within such period shall be deemed a waiver thereof. Failure to appeal a grievance from one level to another within the periods hereafter provided shall also constitute a waiver of the grievance.

Figure 2-8

SAMPLE GRIEVANCE PROCEDURE (continued)

1. Level I—The written grievance, signed by the teacher involved, must be presented to the responsible administrator within agreed upon time limits. The responsible administrator shall meet with the teacher within seven days after receipt of the written grievance and give a written answer to the grievance within five days of the meeting. The teacher has five days in which to either accept the answer or appeal it in writing to the next level.

2. Level II—If the grievance has not been resolved in level I, it then may be processed to level II by presenting the written grievance to the superintendent. The superintendent or his or her designee shall meet within ten days after receipt of the written appeal to discuss the problem with the teacher. Within seven days of the meeting, the superintendent or his or her designee shall submit his or her written answer to the grievant. The teacher has five days in which either to accept the answer or to appeal it in writing to the next level. Such appeal shall be served in the office of the superintendent.

3. Level III—If the grievance has not been resolved at level II, the grievance may be presented to the school board for consideration. The school board reserves the right to review or not to review the grievance but must make that decision within 15 days after receipt of the written appeal. In the event the school board chooses to review a grievance, the board or a committee thereof, within 15 days, shall meet to hear the grievance. After the meeting, the board shall have a maximum of 15 days in which to answer the grievance in writing. If the matter is not resolved at this level, the teacher has five days to either accept the answer or appeal it to arbitration by filing such appeal in the office of the superintendent. The school board reserves the right at its own instance to review any decision under level I or level II of this procedure, provided the school board serves such notice within 15 days after the decision is issued. In the event that the school board reviews a grievance under this subdivision, the school board receives the right to affirm, reverse, or modify such decision.

4. Denial of Grievance—Failure by the school district to issue a decision within the time periods provided herein shall constitute a denial of the grievance, and the teacher may appeal it to the next level. This shall not negate the obligation of the school district to respond in writing at each level of this procedure.

Figure 2–8 (continued)

CHAPTER SUPPLEMENTS

The following chapter supplements are included to illustrate the principles outlined in this chapter.

Contents:

- Model Policy on Negotiations
- Characteristics of a Successful Chief Negotiator
- Suggested Ground Rules for Negotiations
- Sample Grievance Report Form

MODEL POLICY ON NEGOTIATIONS

The board shall negotiate in good faith on appropriate concerns. It shall deal with staff negotiating units openly and fairly and will sincerely endeavor to reach agreement on items being negotiated. Nothing in negotiations shall abridge the board's legal responsibilities nor will any staff member's rights and privileges under statutes be impaired.

It is the intent of the board to utilize negotiations procedures that achieve the following goals:

1. To guarantee employees that they will receive a thorough study of their proposals as well as full consideration in reaching decisions related thereto.

2. To provide an orderly means for resolving disputes.

3. To meet all legal requirements of the state statutes.

The board, as duly constituted representatives of the people and as the agent of the state, is legally responsible for the conduct of public education in the district, and its authority to make final decisions is provided for by law and may not be delegated or abdicated.

CHARACTERISTICS OF A SUCCESSFUL CHIEF NEGOTIATOR

- Experience in labor contract negotiating
- Sound knowledge of labor law and the negotiating process
- Understanding of current contract provisions and operating procedures
- Ability to draft clear contract language
- Capacity to maintain discipline within the negotiating team
- An instinct for anticipating problems
- Patience, stamina, and stability
- Listening skills
- Controlled temper
- Ability to say no and mean it
- Sense of humor
- Absolute integrity and credibility

SUGGESTED GROUND RULES FOR NEGOTIATIONS

- The location of all negotiation sessions should be determined in advance (sometimes a neutral setting is advantageous to both parties). If cost is involved in securing an appropriate meeting place, responsibility for the expense should be agreed upon.

- Time parameters for all sessions should be established in advance. It is often beneficial to agree that no session will continue beyond 5:00 P.M. in the absence of prior special agreement. If meetings are to be conducted during working hours some mutual understanding must be reached regarding pay for participants during their regular duty hours.

- The composition and size of each negotiating team should be agreed upon mutually before the initial session.

- Unless a statutory open meeting is required by law, specific agreements should be reached regarding who may attend negotiation sessions (such as third-party observers, media representatives, alternates, and so on).

- .To the extent possible, the agenda for each subsequent meeting should be agreed to at the conclusion of the previous session.

- The party suggesting a new or revised contract clause should be required to explain the purpose of the proposed change.

- Each party should sign off (initial) the language of every contract clause as soon as agreement is reached.

- Subsequent meetings always should be scheduled in timely fashion. An indefinite or open-ended schedule of negotiating sessions is detrimental to the productivity of the process.

GRIEVANCE REPORT FORM
(SAMPLE)

Name _____School/building _____

Date grievance occurred _____

Statement of facts

Specific provisions of agreement allegedly violated

Particular relief sought

Date _____   _____
                        (Signature of grievant)

3

Shirt-Sleeve Solutions to Special Personnel Problems

Despite whatever overall plans are developed to promote and enhance positive personnel management, there are inevitable nitty-gritty, day-to-day personal and interpersonal problems within every school which can undermine such efforts and create havoc in terms of morale, climate, and productivity.

These special personnel problems can arise at any time in any school and usually involve individuals or small groups. Nevertheless, they can infect and affect the entire staff and the total school operation.

The goal of good management is to reduce or eliminate localized problem areas in ways that help the individuals involved perform more effectively and that contribute to keeping the school program on track while fostering schoolwide harmony and progress.

This chapter outlines a variety of concrete means that administrators can employ in dealing with the most common pockets of special personnel problems that can make a good school go sour in a short time.

ESSENTIALS FOR EASING INTERNAL STAFF SQUABBLES

When all employees feel good about themselves and their fellow workers, the organization functions smoothly. However, when antagonisms, jealousies, rivalries, or personality conflicts arise among even a few staff members, the entire program becomes vulnerable.

Some hostilities or confrontations are normal and must be expected in any human institution. Nevertheless, organizational leaders cannot afford to ignore such situations and hope that they will resolve themselves. They seldom do.

When conflicts occur within the staff at any level, administrators should deal with them directly and in ways that enable all parties involved to save face and feel support.

In seeking to settle squabbles, avoid dissension, and improve the sense of community within the school, the first task of the administrator in charge is to identify the sources of recurring conflict. Some of the most prevalent causes of interpersonal staff conflict or dissension include those shown in Figure 3–1.

Regardless of cause, the primary role of administrators in preventing or handling interpersonal staff disputes is threefold, as depicted in Figure 3–2.

In addition to the primary approaches, school leaders can tap a continuum of strife strategies, including the following:

- Provide presence—get out from behind the desk and deal directly with people-to-people problems.
- Hold personal conferences with conflicting staff members.
- Engage neutral staff members to serve as buffers between disputing parties.
- Design faculty meetings that emphasize ways to bring people together, perhaps setting aside time for discussion of personal issues.
- Separate disputing parties through scheduling and room assignment.
- Issue direct orders to cease and desist divisive bickering and behavior.
- Openly acknowledge that all employees have the freedom or right to their feelings.
- Arrange for group therapy where appropriate.
- Make referrals to psychological services as needed.
- Press for transfers of incompatible personnel.

NO-NONSENSE DO'S AND DON'TS FOR DEALING WITH ABSENTEEISM

Naturally, some absenteeism must be expected within any human institution. In some organizations, however, excessive and chronic absenteeism can become a major problem and a primary source of lowered morale, reduced efficiency, and increased costs.

Some schools and school systems subtly develop an "absenteeism culture" where attendance is taken lightly and almost any excuse to miss work is eagerly embraced by employees.

Excessive absenteeism is both a symptom and a cause of an unhealthy school or work environment and should be addressed directly and systematically by all administrators and supervisors involved. It is no more important to focus concen-

```
┌─────────────────────────────┐        ┌─────────────────────────────┐
│      Individual Factors      │        │        Group Factors         │
│                              │        │                              │
│  Loneliness                  │        │  Social cliques              │
│  Feelings of inadequacy      │        │  Barriers of mistrust        │
│  Guilt feelings              │        │  Sensitivity among levels of │
│  Midlife crises              │        │     employees                │
│  Frustration                 │        │  Artificial relationships    │
│  Sense of meaningless        │        │  Little community of feelings│
│  Sense of being exploited    │        │     among professional peers │
│  Loss of identity            │        │  Prejudice or stereotyping   │
│  Personal or family problems │        │                              │
│  Burnout                     │        │                              │
└─────────────────────────────┘        └─────────────────────────────┘
```

```
            ┌─────────────────────────────────────┐
            │         Institutional Factors        │
            │                                      │
            │  Physical isolation                  │
            │  Pressures for conformity            │
            │  Administrative manipulation         │
            │  Limited sanctioned channels for     │
            │     venting hostility or anger       │
            │  Discriminatory practices            │
            │  Labor–management disputes           │
            └─────────────────────────────────────┘
```

Figure 3–1

```
┌─────────────────────────────────────────────────────────────────────┐
│                                                                       │
│                    DISPUTE MANAGEMENT MODEL                           │
│                                                                       │
│  In situations involving interpersonal staff conflicts, officials     │
│  should serve as:                                                     │
│     1. Models—Exemplify self-understanding and helping others         │
│        through facing oneself.                                        │
│     2. Mediators—Strive for acceptance of differences and mutual      │
│        respect.                                                        │
│     3. Mood Setters—Stress team building and collaboration as         │
│        earmarks of professional conduct.                              │
│                                                                       │
│                         Figure 3–2                                    │
│                                                                       │
└─────────────────────────────────────────────────────────────────────┘
```

trated efforts on improving student attendance than it is to take the necessary steps to maintain a positive record of staff attendance where needed.

In recent times, some schools have experienced increasing staff attendance problems as a result of (1) negotiated leave provisions (sick leave, emergency leave, personal leave, and so on), (2) the attitudes and work habits of a new breed of young teachers, and (3) increasing numbers of teachers and other employees approaching retirement age.

Analysis of many situations in which an unusually high incidence of employee absenteeism occurs in schools reveals some fairly common elements or patterns such as the following:

- The more contracted leave days that are provided, the more days are likely to be used.
- There are often more absences on the part of employees who live long distances from the school.
- Women workers tend to have higher absentee rates.
- Attendance is often highest (sometimes perfect) on paydays.
- Mondays tend to be bad days for attendance (this is often not as true in school settings, however, as in the private sector).
- Sometimes, absentee rates increase as retirement nears.

Some of the most frequent causes of staff attendance problems include:

- Low morale
  Morale and attendance within the school tend to interact together and can create a vicious cycle, as depicted below:

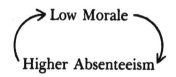

- Substandard working conditions
- Misunderstanding of the intent of contractual provisions
- Inflexible schedules
- Poor personnel practices (such as inattentive and insensitive management)

Many districts have found that the most effective staff attendance plans employ a diplomatic, low-key approach.

The initial step in developing strategies for improving employee attendance is simply accurate data gathering and recordkeeping. It is essential for administrators and supervisors to have accurate attendance information and a realistic sense of existing absenteeism patterns in order to diagnose where any problems are and to prescribe remedial measures where needed. A sample format for recording and reporting attendance information on a districtwide basis appears in Figure 3–3. Repeated experiences in business and industry as well as in public enterprises have demonstrated that the following are the three most markedly successful (result-producing) techniques for combating excessive absenteeism:

1. Initiating accurate recordkeeping and documentation.
2. Monitoring absenteeism, recording trends, identifying chronic problem areas, and concentrating on offending employees.
3. Requiring all personnel to report absences directly and personally to their immediate supervisors rather than to an automatic recording or Code-A-Phone™ device.

In addition to the basics of attendance management identified above, the list of tested do's and don'ts in Figure 3–4 can aid administrators in turning around even abysmal absenteeism situations and establishing norms of high attendance rates within any school setting.

A PRACTICAL PRESCRIPTION FOR HELPING STAFF MEMBERS WHO HAVE DRINKING OR DRUG PROBLEMS

A modern view of positive personnel management requires some proactive measures to reclaim valuable human resources which might otherwise be lost due to drug abuse among staff members. This section lays out a sound and sensible approach for helping employees with drinking and other drug-related problems.

Any incidence of alcohol or drug abuse among staff members can pose a particularly delicate personnel problem. Whenever a drug-related problem develops involving any school employee, the manager in charge must be concerned with all of the following aspects of what can be a very sensitive situation:

- The employee's well-being and future career
- The possible effects on students
- The maintenance of an effective instructional program within the classroom
- The total school climate and staff interpersonal relations
- The school's image and relations with the community

Most effective school personnel management programs now encompass a well-developed and comprehensive plan for dealing with problems caused by chemical dependency on the part of either students or staff members. The goals of such a plan should include:

ANNUAL SICK LEAVE SUMMARY

	1979–80	1981–82
Personal illness	2074	1490
Family illness	190	171
Family/other death	64	43
Emergency leave	86	74
Total days used	2414	1778
FTE teachers	385.3	341
Days leave/teacher	6.26	5.21

TEACHER ABSENCES BY DAYS OF THE WEEK

Monday	432.0 days	(no school on 6 Mondays)
Tuesday	443.0 days	(no school on 3 Tuesdays)
Wednesday	427.5 days	(no school on 3 Wednesdays)
Thursday	404.0 days	(no school on 11 Thursdays)
Friday	381.0 days	(no school on 13 Fridays)
TOTAL	2092.5 days	

TEACHER ABSENCES BY MONTH
1980–81

August (2 school days)	0.0 days
September (17 school days)	87.5 days
October (20 school days)	163.5 days
November (18 school days)	146.5 days
December (15 school days)	165.0 days
January (18 school days)	156.5 days
TOTAL	719.0 days

Figure 3–3

DO'S AND DON'TS OF ATTENDANCE IMPROVEMENT

Do

Provide for adequate accumulation of sick leave.

Focus on teacher presence.

Publicize absenteeism trends and profiles and show costs involved.

Provide each staff member with a printout of his or her attendance record annually.

Send get-well cards, visit staff members who are ill, and welcome returning teachers following each absence.

Consider allocating funds saved from reduced substitute costs for building use as an attendance incentive.

Consider paying teachers for unused sick leave through severance pay provision or other arrangements.

Recognize outstanding attendance records.

Don't

Ignore any absence.

Neglect to stress the importance of attendance in preemployment interviews.

Maintain inadequate or inaccurate records.

Overlook the importance of exemplifying position attendance patterns.

Omit attendance as a factor in professional performance appraisal.

Penalize staff members with good attendance records by requiring them to cover for absent colleagues.

Figure 3–4

1. Establishment of a strong and unequivocal commitment on the part of the school board and administration to an ongoing program of education, counseling, and referral services related to chemical dependency.

2. Provision for immediate counseling and referral services to chemically dependent students or employees.

3. Development of a trained cadre of staff whose services and skills are available to students and staff with chemical dependency problems.

4. Initiation of a systemwide educational program, appropriate at all levels, to inform students and staff of the causes, symptoms, and treatment of chemical dependency.

To achieve these goals, the following ten-point action plan has been effective in a variety of schools and school systems throughout the country:

1. Adopt a firm, forthright policy statement regarding chemical dependency and drug abuse (see Figure 3–5).

2. Orient the staff and community to the concept of alcoholism and other kinds of chemical dependency as both an individual and a family illness.

3. Employ a chemical dependency counselor or chemical health specialist (see sample position description in Figure 3–6).

4. Provide for easily accessible counseling and referral services. These services should include:

   • Evaluating employees who may have the disease and making recommendations.

   • Providing or arranging for individual and family counseling services as needed.

   • Arranging for in-patient and out-patient treatment when indicated.

   • Establishing contact groups and continuing therapy for recovering employees.

5. Initiate interventions where necessary and appropriate.

6. Implement appropriate staff development and public information programs.

7. Make available employee medical insurance programs that cover the cost of treatment for chemical dependency.

8. Develop support groups for students, employees, and family members.

9. Provide awareness training to help all staff members in receiving and relating to recovering employees.

10. Maintain strict confidentiality in all incidents of chemical dependency problems.

This approach to handling and helping staff members with drug-related problems is a far cry from the traditional response to such issues, which was usually

POLICY ON CHEMICAL DEPENDENCY

The school district recognizes chemical dependency as a treatable illness. District employees who are so diagnosed shall receive the same consideration and opportunity for treatment that is extended to employees with other types of illness. On the basis of medical certification, employees with the illness of chemical dependency shall qualify for the same health service benefits that are provided for other medically certified illnesses.

The district's concern with chemical dependency is limited to its effects on the employee's job performance. For purposes of this policy, chemical dependency is defined as an illness in which an employee's consumption of mood-altering chemicals repeatedly interferes with his or her job performance and/or adversely affects his or her health.

Supervisors will implement this policy in such a manner that no employee with chemical dependency will have his or her job security or promotional opportunity affected either by the diagnosis itself or by the employee's request for treatment.

If the employee refuses to accept diagnosis and treatment or fails to respond to treatment, and the result of such refusal or failure is such that his or her job performance continues to be affected, it will be handled in the same way as similar refusal or treatment failure would be handled for any other illness. Implementation of this policy will not require or result in any special regulations, privileges, or exemptions from the standard administrative practice applicable to job performance requirements.

The confidential nature of the medical records of employees with chemical dependency will be preserved in the same manner as for all other medical records.

The purpose of this policy is to encourage recognition, early intervention, and subsequent support for the chemically dependent employee.

Figure 3–5

CHEMICAL HEALTH SPECIALIST

Responsibilities:

- Assist in making referrals and interventions for staff and students.
- Coordinate the work of Al-A-Teens support and growth groups, participating actively as needed.
- Be responsible for working with staff in developing and implementing preventive strategies.
- Plan and provide continuing in-service training for appropriate staff in the areas of chemical dependency and related mental health issues.
- Be responsible for parent education and awareness programs at all levels.
- Work directly with students and staff and serve as a resource to classroom activities.
- Act as liaison with related community agencies.

Figure 3—6

immediate dismissal. The strategies recommended not only provide a more humane way to deal with a very human problem, but they also offer some means of reclaiming valuable human resources with unique talents in which the school has often made a substantial investment and which would otherwise be lost.

GUIDELINES FOR TEACHERS'
POLITICAL AND RELIGIOUS ACTIVITIES

Although dramatically different from the problems caused by employees suffering from chemical dependency, some equally sticky problems can arise from staff members who become overly zealous in pursuing individual religious or political activities both inside and outside the classroom.

Although principals and other administrators should foster a climate of academic freedom and advocate or protect the rights of all employees to their own private opinions and convictions, internal and external problems can arise when staff members exceed recognized restraints in promoting specific political or religious views.

 n most communities, parents and other citizens are extremely sensitive to any hint of inappropriate actions on the part of teachers or other staff members to capitalize on or exploit students as a captive audience with special vulnerability for purposes of indoctrination to any particular bias or belief.

In order to prevent such situations, the board and administration should take pains to develop specific policies, regulations, and guidelines that spell out appropriate limits for staff activities related to religion or politics within the classroom, while protecting the individual employee's freedom of thought. When such guides are exceeded or blatantly violated, appropriate disciplinary action (reprimand, suspension, or dismissal) should be imposed as swiftly as possible.

The model policies and guidelines in Figures 3–7A through 7D have helped many districts in precluding or defusing volatile situations involving inappropriate religious or political activities by employees.

The sample policies, guidelines, and regulations enumerated in Figures 3–7A through 7D can assist in defining desirable and undesirable practices and activities related to religion and politics in any school.

HOW TO EASE THE PAIN OF LAYOFFS

Throughout the 1970s and early 1980s, school districts across the country have been confronted with the difficult and sometimes devastating task of reducing personnel and placing valued staff members, both licensed and classified, on unrequested leave. Managing this painful process requires some new skills for many veteran administrators.

Obviously, there is no simple formula for effecting a reduction in force (RIF) without hurting individuals and the total system to some extent. There are,

STAFF ETHICS:
RELIGIOUS OR
POLITICAL ACTIVITY

An effective educational program requires the services of men and women of integrity, high ideals, and human understanding. To maintain and promote these essentials, all employees are expected to maintain high standards in their school relationships. These standards include restraint from using school contacts and privileges to promote partisan politics, sectarian religious views, or selfish propaganda of any kind.

Figure 3–7A

GUIDELINES REGARDING
ACCEPTABLE AND UNACCEPTABLE
PRACTICES RELATED TO
RELIGIOUS ACTIVITY
IN THE SCHOOL

1. The school's position regarding religion should be instructional, not devotional.
2. Teachers may expose students to a variety of religious beliefs but should refrain from imposing any specific view.
3. Teachers may teach about various religions but should refrain from any attempt to indoctrinate or convert pupils to any specific religion.
4. The school may sponsor the study of religion but not the practice of any specific religious doctrine.

Figure 3–7B

STAFF PARTICIPATION IN
POLITICAL ACTIVITIES

The school board recognizes that employees have the same fundamental responsibilities and privileges as other citizens. Among these are campaigning for an elective public office and holding an elected or appointed public office.

Any employee who intends to campaign for an elected public office shall notify the superintendent in writing, at the earliest possible time, of the office he or she intends to seek when participation would interfere with the employee's performance of duties.

In connection with campaigning, no employee shall use school system facilities, equipment, or supplies; nor shall the employee discuss the campaign with school personnel or students during the work day; nor shall the employee use any time during the working day for campaign purposes.

Figure 3—7C

REGULATIONS REGARDING
POLITICAL ACTIVITY
IN THE SCHOOL

1. The circulation of literature for or against any candidate for political office through the facilities of the school shall be prohibited, except at public meetings and as distribution may be required by postal regulations.
2. Employees of the school district shall not participate in political activities during the school day.
3. Employees of the school district shall not solicit, enlist, or organize students for political activities during the regular school day.
4. Equipment or supplies of the school district shall not be used in the preparation or distribution of political materials at any time.
5. If candidates are invited to speak to students during or after school hours, all candidates for a given office shall be extended an invitation to appear. Teachers shall be responsible for arranging equal time and opportunity for all concerned.

Figure 3—7D

however, a number of practical measures that can be undertaken to minimize the pain.

Implementing a program of staff retrenchment should be more than a numbers game. It can and should be a human process.

Whenever layoffs occur or are imminent, school leaders should consider the impact both on the system and on the individuals involved. Some of the damaging effects that a reduction in force can have on the school or the school system include:

- Lower morale
- Strained relationships
- Reduced performance
- Interstaff conflicts
- Carryover into the classroom

Of even greater concern in some instances is the potential impact on affected staff members. Most employees who are involved in terminations or unrequested leaves experience a grief cycle of guilt, anger, depression, and other emotions similar to those associated with the death of a loved one. The primary reactions of teachers and others who face unexpected unemployment in such circumstances are most commonly related to fear and stress.

Fear

- Of loss of economic security
- Of loss of identity
- Of loss of stability in their lives
- Of loss of retirement and other benefits
- Of loss of future plans and dreams
- Of change and the unknown

Stress

- Personal
- Emotional
- Physical

All of these factors should be appreciated and considered by those in charge of engineering a program of staff reduction.

A Checklist for Carrying Out a Reduction in Force (RIF) Program

The practical suggestions described below have succeeded in many districts in minimizing the negative impact of a reduction in force, in easing the trauma for those involved, in preserving a human focus during a difficult period, and in maintaining the quality of relationships and performance within the school:

☑ Plan ahead—Provide projected staff needs (on a department-by-department basis if feasible) as early as possible.

☑ Don't keep secrets—Be open and honest regarding cutback plans.

☑ Publicize all pertinent data (projected enrollments, budget figures, seniority lists, and so on).

☑ Communicate the mechanics of the process to all staff members.

☑ Involve staff in developing budget reduction recommendations.

☑ Keep the educational program paramount throughout the process.

☑ Do not use the RIF process as an opportunity to dump undesirables.

☑ Humanize and personalize the notification process as much as possible (see sample letter in Figure 3–8, page 69).

☑ Consider appointment of an RIF coordinator.

☑ Attempt to distribute notices of placement on unrequested leave at a time that creates the least turmoil. Notices should be delivered in person and in private.

☑ Promote maximal use of early retirement, general leaves (leaves to explore alternative careers, and so on), job sharing, tandem teaching, and part-time positions in order to minimize the number of terminated personnel.

☑ Urge retiring teachers to give early notice.

☑ Provide out-placement services as soon as possible.

☑ Be diligent in providing references and letters of recommendation.

☑ Provide information about outstanding teachers affected by layoffs to other school districts that may be in need of qualified personnel.

☑ Attempt to be flexible in allowing terminated teachers to participate in job interviews during the regular working day.

☑ Don't take personally the natural anger and resentment expressed by terminated employees.

☑ Use legal counsel as needed. Strictly adhere to due-process requirements and follow all existing policies in good faith.

☑ Sponsor mid-career change workshops for affected employees (see sample program in Figure 3–9, page 70).

☑ Continue to show you care about the affected employees in the aftermath. Keep staff members actively involved.

☑ Focus on a healing process. Emphasize opportunities for growth.

☑ Work with the local teachers' organization to formulate a program of saving some positions through voluntary, tax-free contributions from employees unaffected by layoffs. Sample procedures for such a program, entitled "Save Our Available Resources" (SOAR), are outlined in Figure 3–10, page 71.

Obviously, none of the measures described above can make a layoff process in any school totally painless. In addition, efforts to humanize the process result in a more complex, difficult, and time-consuming undertaking. Nevertheless, in terms of maintaining long-term morale, showing genuine concern for respected staff members who are victims of the circumstances, and preserving the quality of relationships among remaining employees, these efforts can be an invaluable investment of personnel management time.

ANYWHERE PUBLIC SCHOOLS   INDEPENDENT DISTRICT 100
1234 MAIN STREET, ANYWHERE, U.S.A. 54321
200-555-1000

I wanted to express my personal concern to you in addition to the formal notice you are receiving today of your intended placement on unrequested leave at the end of the current school year. Although we have been touched to a limited extent by enrollment decline reductions since 1978, this is the first time in three years that we have had to make cuts of the scope currently under way. In all of the years that I have been doing this, I have never become blase or viewed it as a necessary ritual because it is a most unpleasant action, regardless of whether one is the initiator or the recipient.

I appreciate greatly the years of time and effort you have contributed to the students of Anywhere and to the district as a whole. This is hardly an appropriate way to show my appreciation, but I hope that you recognize the dire nature of our circumstances and the reluctance with which we carry out this action. I assure you that we are pursuing every possible means to develop additional funding for the school district. It is my hope that we will be able to make further restorations in staff over the ensuing months and that you will be one of those.

In the meantime, if I can assist you in any way, whether professionally or personally, now or in the future, please contact me. We will make every effort between now and the start of the school year to find a way to bring you back into the district, ideally in the same status in which you are currently serving.

This is not a happy day for the district, and I know particularly how devastating it must be for you. My thoughts are very much with you and your colleagues as you receive these letters, and they will stay with you in the weeks and months ahead.

Sincerely,

M. E. Smith

M. E. Smith, Ph.D.
Superintendent

MES:nk

Figure 3–8

IS THERE LIFE AFTER EDUCATION?

(Mid-Career Change Workshop)

Agenda

1. Coping with stress

2. The job search process

3. Résumé writing

4. The realities of the job market (representatives from employers interested in hiring teachers)

5. Panel of former educators sharing career transition experiences

6. Questions

Figure 3–9

SOAR PROCEDURES

Introduction

Approximately $17,000 has been raised through staff contributions to assist in underwriting the cost of retaining certain terminated personnel on a substitute teacher basis. Procedures for implementing the plan follows.

Upon completing a detailed profile of our employment of substitute teachers last year, we found that we need six substitutes for 155 days.

We shall employ six permanent subs for next year, from among those licensed personnel who have been placed on unrequested leave, for 170 days. We estimate that at least 15 of those 170 days of employment, as well as the cost of the fringe benefits specified on the letter of assignment, would be covered by the contributions to SOAR. The other 155 days of employment for the permanent substitutes will be paid out of district funds already budgeted for substitutes next year.

Personnel

Three teachers with elementary certification and three teachers with secondary certification shall be hired as permanent substitutes. In the case of the three elementary people, we shall recall in order of seniority three teachers who are currently working in an elementary school assignment, two of whom must have NKP or K–6 certification and one of whom should have certification in other specialties such as physical education or music. In the case of the three secondary people, we shall recall in order of seniority three teachers who are currently working in a secondary school assignment but no two of whom have exactly the same areas of licensure. The intent is to provide the district with permanent substitutes who can work in as many subject areas as possible.

Figure 3–10

CHAPTER SUPPLEMENTS

The following chapter supplements are included to illustrate the principles outlined in this chapter.

Contents:

- Sample Absence Verification Form
- Sample Physician's Sick Leave Verification Form
- Sample Absence Reporting Instructions
- Model Policy on "Conflict of Interests"
- Memo Soliciting Early Retirement Notification (Example)

SAMPLE ABSENCE VERIFICATION FORM

Name _____ Date _____

School/building _____

This is to certify that I did not work on the following dates:

_____
(Specify if less than full working day)

Reason for absence (check one)

_____ 1. Personal illness (nature of illness) _____
Was a doctor consulted? _____ Was hospitalization required? _____

_____ 2. Illness of immediate or close family member

_____ 3. Death of immediate or close family member

_____ 4. Injured on the job

_____ 5. Emergency leave (please explain) _____

_____ 6. Vacation

_____ 7. Professional leave (attach approved application)

_____ 8. Other (please specify) _____
If 2 or 3 is checked above, give name, address, and relationship of
the family member:

Name _____ Relationship _____

Address _____

I hereby request the granting of the day(s) of absence designated above in
accord with the leave provisions of this school district.

_____
(Employee's signature)

Responsible administrator _____

ABSENCE: Deduct from sick leave _____
Deduct from pay _____
Do not deduct from sick leave _____

SAMPLE PHYSICIAN'S SICK LEAVE VERIFICATION FORM

To Physician

Your patient, _____, an employee of School District #_____,
has claimed sick leave for the period _____through _____.
Verification of disability is required to make this payment. Please respond to the
following questions regarding the sick leave claim by your patient:

1. Nature of disability (describe)
2. On what date(s) did you examine the patient?
3. Can you verify that the patient was disabled on the dates claimed?
4. Has the employee recovered?
5. (a) In the event the patient remains disabled, what is your estimate of
       when he or she will be able to return to work?

   (b) In such event, when do you anticipate examining the patient again?
6. Other relevant information

_____
(Physician's signature)
_____
(Date)

SAMPLE ABSENCE REPORTING INSTRUCTIONS

Where a recording system is used for reporting absences, the following kinds of directions can be helpful in expediting the process and establishing uniform procedures.

Code-A-Phone™ #_____   Personnel office #_____
When reporting an absence, please give the following information:

1. Name
2. Building/school
3. Grade level or subject
4. Reason for absence

The recording device will be in service between 4:30 P.M. and 6:30 A.M. daily. Emergency absences that occur after 6:30 A.M. may be reported to the personnel office. Call your building by 2:00 P.M. daily, when absent, to inform principal of whether or not you will be returning the next school day.

MODEL POLICY ON CONFLICT OF INTERESTS

In addition to problems involving questionable religious or political activity, some communities experience sensitive situations in which school personnel become involved in commercial ventures—selling encyclopedias, providing private tutoring, sponsoring student tours, and so on—which may exploit the teacher–pupil relationship and violate professional ethics. The model policy below suggests one way to avoid or deal with this kind of special personnel problem.

No employee shall engage in or have a financial interest, directly or indirectly, in any activity that conflicts or raises a reasonable question of conflict with his or her duties and responsibilities.

Employees shall not engage in work of any type where the source of information concerning customer, client, or employee originates from information obtained through the school system.

MEMO SOLICITING EARLY RETIREMENT NOTIFICATION
(EXAMPLE)

Memo To: Certified Staff

Subject: Early Notification of Retirement

The purpose of this memo is to encourage any of you who are considering retirement at the end of the current school year to submit <u>early notification</u> of this intent.

First, we are all too familiar with the anxieties our colleagues face when they are placed on proposed unrequested leave and final unrequested leave—and then, in some cases, reinstated or recalled at a later date. You could help avoid some of these anxieties by declaring your intent to retire by February 1 of the year in which you wish to retire. Such action on your part would immeasurably reduce the anxiety of many ... and would also allow the staffing of the schools for the subsequent year to proceed in a manner much less disruptive to the individuals who must necessarily be transferred to other buildings or assignments.

Second, we are all aware of the financial insecurities faced by the district. One way the district can recoup some funds is through the Teacher Mobility Program for Early Retirement Incentives. Any application to this program must be submitted to the district no later than February 1. Such application does <u>not</u> commit an individual to retirement but does allow the district to possibly recover a portion of early retirement severance funds expended.

Please give serious consideration to declaring your intention to retire by February 1 so that an application for early retirement incentives can be set in motion. The teacher then has until June 1 to submit a formal written resignation, which only then can be acted on by the school board. Before June 1 the teacher may withdraw the declaration of intention to retire since this does not become final until the school board has officially accepted a written resignation.

_____   _____
(President, Local Teachers' Organization)   (Director of Personnel)

4

Real-World Ways to Build Better Staff Morale

Morale is the elusive element within any organization that may spell disaster or success in terms of attaining institutional goals. When morale is high, things hum while progress and productivity advance hand in hand. When morale is low, the organization limps along with sporadic performance and spotty progress.

In basic terms, morale is simply the way employees feel about themselves, their work, their work place, and their overall working life. Staff attitudes toward these areas are key forcing factors in personal performance. In the school setting, maximizing and maintaining high staff morale is one of the fundamental tasks and objectives of positive personnel management.

Productive staff relations constitute the first condition for a successful school. Conversely, troubled relations within the school can lead to acting out on the part of teachers and other employees, often manifested in chronic complaints, divisive behavior, and conscious or unconscious sabotaging of the school's program. Building better staff morale becomes a crucial responsibility for school administrators at all levels.

The remainder of this chapter offers a full spectrum of specific suggestions for morale betterment, which can be put to use in any school situation, large or small.

HOW TO CONDUCT A MORALE SURVEY

An important first step in addressing morale issues directly is to assess the existing climate of staff attitudes, feelings, and perceptions. This can be done informally through interviews and observations or more formally by conducting some form of structured survey. The latter, more systematic approach can be targeted at the district, building, or departmental level.

Some systems have had significant success with a comprehensive districtwide assessment of employee opinions and concerns. Where this approach is utilized, it is essential that all staff members (certified and classified) have an opportunity to respond and that the integrity of confidentiality is respected without question.

Figures 4–1 and 4–2 present real-life examples of a model morale survey form and the format one district has employed to report the findings of its assessment of employee attitudes.

In order for a formal survey instrument to serve as a truly effective tool for morale management, pains must be taken to report the results fully, honestly, and accurately to all respondents and other interested parties. Of course, it is equally important for the reported results to be acted upon in some visible fashion. Usually, the findings will point toward certain actions related to district-level operations and some that can only be addressed at the building level by the principal. In all cases, it is advisable to consider some form of periodic follow-up to identify areas of progress as well as pockets of continuing concern.

ESSENTIAL BUILDING BLOCKS FOR BETTER MORALE

Regardless of the outcome of surveying any particular school situation, there are certain general components that are necessary ingredients for a positive, overall morale picture in any setting. Successful school managers must be familiar with the basics that contribute to the quality of working life for all employees and, ultimately, to a productive climate throughout the school.

One of the prerequisites for ensuring a positive working environment is the ability to recognize and appreciate productive attitudes and relationships when they exist. The morale model in Figure 4–3 identifies the kinds of attitudes and behaviors that characterize a state of healthy working relationships, high motivation, and productive performance.

In order to achieve the qualities outlined in Figure 4–3 (page 84), school leaders must understand the cornerstones of concern that serve as a superstructure for maximum morale. These basic components are depicted in the building block diagram in Figure 4–4. In order to achieve a well-rounded atmosphere of positive espirit de corps within a school or an entire district, each of the broad areas identified must be addressed in specific ways.

Incentive concerns represent many of the intangible elements of the work place that most workers admit are crucial to their continuing satisfaction and maximal output. These factors are often more important than salary or fringe benefits in determining employee attitudes and contentment. Successful provision for the incentive concerns of staff members usually rests squarely on the personality and style of the leaders involved.

MODEL MORALE SURVEY

Purpose of This Survey

This questionnaire is the result of approximately 275 interviews conducted in this district. It gives you the opportunity to express your opinions about the district or school matters. We hope it touches upon all areas of concern. If you feel something of importance to you has been missed, feel free to use the comments section at the end of the questionnaire.

How to Fill in the Survey

There are no right or wrong answers. All we want is your personal opinion based on your knowledge and experience.

Stay anonymous.

Do not sign your name. We do not wish to identify individuals, only groups and schools or locations.

Key

SA = Strongly Agree
TA = Tend to Agree
TD = Tend to Disagree
SD = Strongly Disagree

Circle the choice that best fits your opinion.

1. The district administrative staff's decisions seem fair.   SA   TA   TD   SD

2. In general, I approve of district administrative policies.   SA   TA   TD   SD

3. I have little opportunity to express my ideas to administration.   SA   TA   TD   SD

4. I am treated like a professional at all times.   SA   TA   TD   SD

5. I am rarely told whether or not I am doing good work.   SA   TA   TD   SD

6. There is too much friction between professional and nonprofessional staff.   SA   TA   TD   SD

7. My immediate supervisor is responsive to my needs.   SA   TA   TD   SD

8. The administrative staff does a good job handling our complaints.   SA   TA   TD   SD

Figure 4–1

9. My immediate supervisor shows initiative in seeking ways to help us in our work. SA TA TD SD

10. The rules and regulations established by the administration make sense to me. SA TA TD SD

11. As far as they affect me, the decisions made by the administration are fair and equitable. SA TA TD SD

12. Our salary system adequately rewards outstanding work. SA TA TD SD

13. I think my work performance is judged fairly. SA TA TD SD

14. I think the school administration does all it can to help build an effective educational program. SA TA TD SD

15. My principal tries to get my ideas about things. SA TA TD SD

16. I would prefer a different work assignment from the one I now have. SA TA TD SD

17. We are kept well informed about matters affecting us in our work. SA TA TD SD

18. It is often difficult to get assistance when I need it. SA TA TD SD

19. In general, I approve of school administrative policies. SA TA TD SD

20. I have little opportunity to express my opinions to administration. SA TA TD SD

21. The procedures for judging my performance are helpful to me in improving my work. SA TA TD SD

Figure 4–1 *(continued)*

Morale Survey Report

Fall, 1980

During the Spring of 1979, the St. Louis Park Public Schools initiated a comprehensive staff morale study which has become recognized as a model for school districts throughout the state and beyond.

This extensive survey, involving all licensed and classified personnel, was conducted by Ross Brouse (University of Minnesota doctoral candidate) at no cost to the district. The techniques used in the study included in-depth, personal interviews with representative staff members from all levels and the completion of a detailed survey instrument by all employees.

Preliminary findings of the study were reported to the staff at building level meetings during the 1979-80 school year and a complete formal report of the results was presented to the School Board last Spring.

The responses of the participants clustered around five (5) major factors:

(1) Perception of District administration
(2) Community relations
(3) Growth opportunities
(4) Interpersonal relationships with administrators
(5) Supervisory relationships

The report which follows provides a capsule analysis of the most significant outcomes of the study according to the following breakdown of the survey results:

- **General Factors** — Items receiving the most significant weightings based on a factor analysis of results from all respondents.
- **Teacher Results** — Items based on teacher responses only.
- **"Good News"** — Areas appearing to be reasonably satisfactory in terms of fostering/maintaining positive morale.
- **"Bad News"** — Areas needing attention or correction
- **"Rx"** — Recommendations and suggested remedial measures.

The information in this capsule summary and in the full morale study report will be used by the Staff Development/ Self Development Committee and by building and District administrators in forming plans to improve the "teaching/ working climate" for all employees.

Mike Hickey
Superintendent

Figure 4—2

Factors	General Results	Teacher Results
	(The following items received the most significant weightings based on a factor analysis of the results from all respondents)	*(Items based on teacher results only)* A = Agree D = Disagree

Perception of District Administration

General Results:

Mostly Plus
1. Approval of district administration policies (Items 2 and 19)
2. Rules/regulations make sense (Item 11)
3. Administration's decisions seem fair (Items 1 and 10)

Teacher Results:

Mostly Plus
1. Treated like a professional (Item 4, 58.4% A)
2. Administration does good job handling complaints (Item 8, 54.1% A)
3. Administration does all it can to build effective educational programs (Item 14, 56.5% A)
4. I'm kept informed of matters affecting work (Items 49 and 17, 60.7% and 58.9% A)
5. Administration makes right decisions (Item 25, 63.6% A)
6. Administration is willing to consider our ideas (Item 51, 58.6% A)
7. Information issued to the press accurately represents me and the district (Item 52, 52.5% A)

Mostly Minus
1. I can trust district Administration more as time goes by (Item 26, 60.3% D)

Community Relations

General Results:

Mostly Plus
1. Parents understand goals of the school (Item 60)
2. Administration in my school does an adequate job involving the community (Item 64)
3. Parents support the school (Item 61)

Teacher Results:

Mostly Plus
1. People in the community are "education" oriented (Item 56, 78.6% A)
2. People in the community would be interested in early childhood and parent education (Item 65, 78.3% A)

Mostly Minus
1. People without school age children are interested in schools (Item 63, 65.7% D)

Growth Opportunities

General Results: NONE APPLICABLE

Teacher Results:

Mostly Plus
1. Work provides ample opportunity for personal growth/development (Item 67, 60.3% A)
2. Salary system encourages growth (Item 68, 52.9% A)
3. I am encouraged to attend conferences/workshops (Item 72, 58.9% A)
4. Leave system adequate to suit my needs (Item 78, 62.4% A)

Mostly Minus
1. Method of performance appraisal is helpful in improving work (Item 70, 51.6% D)
2. District inservice programs are relevant (Item 76, 63.1% D)
3. I am rewarded for self-improvement (Item 77, 57.6% D)

Interpersonal Relationships with Administrators

General Results:

Mostly Plus
1. Opportunity to express opinions to administrators (Items 3 and 20)

Mostly Minus
1. Rarely told whether or not I'm doing good work (Item 5)

Teacher Results:

Mostly Plus
1. Too much friction between professional and nonprofessional staff (Item 6, 89.6%)
2. Little opportunity to express ideas to administration (Item 3, 57% D)
3. Difficult to get assistance when needed (Item 18, 75.3% D)
4. Employee benefits don't meet needs (Item 22, 74.6% D)
5. Difficult to communicate problems up the line (Item 40, 63% D)
6. Don't understand how performance is evaluated (Item 50, 75.7% D)

Mostly Minus
1. Rarely told whether or not I'm doing good work (Item 23, 58.6% A)
2. Administration seems to lack interest in personal welfare of faculty (Item 30, 66% A)
3. More attention seems to be paid to administrative matters than educational matters (Item 31, 68.6% A)

Supervisory Relationships

General Results:

Mostly Plus
1. Immediate supervisor shows initiative in seeking ways to help (Item 9)
2. Supervisor keeps me informed about matters affecting work (Item 35)

Teacher Results:

Mostly Plus
1. Supervisor is responsive to needs (Item 7, 84.2% A)
2. Performance is judged fairly (Item 13, 85.8% A)
3. Principal tries to get my ideas (Item 15, 85.7% A)
4. Supervisor keeps me informed of matters affecting work (Item 73, 79.6% A)

Mostly Minus
1. Procedures for judging performance are helpful to improving work (Item 21, 51.6% D)

Figure 4–2 *(continued)*

"Good News"

(Although improvement is always possible, the following areas appear to be reasonably satisfactory in terms of fostering/maintaining positive morale")

1. Administrative policies, rules, regulations and decisions
2. Professional treatment
3. Complaint handling
4. Administrative efforts to improve educational programs
5. Internal communications
6. Press information/relations

---

1. Parent understanding, support, and interest
2. Community involvement
3. Community interest in early childhood and parent education

---

1. Leave system
2. Salary system for rewarding improvement
3. Encouragement for attending conferences/workshops

---

1. Performance appraisal process is *understandable*
2. Communication up-the-line
3. Friction is minimal
4. Freedom to express ideas
5. Benefit system

---

1. Supervisor responsiveness and helpfulness
2. Supervisor-staff communication
3. *Fairness* of performance appraisal

"Bad News"

(The survey results identify the following area(s) which need addition/correction:)

1. Distrust of district administration

---

1. Nonparent lack of interest in schools and school programs

---

1. Performance appraisal is *not* perceived as helpful in improving work
2. Inservice programs aren't relevant
3. Lack of rewards (other than salary) for self-improvement

---

1. Staff rarely told whether or not doing good work
2. Administration perceived as disinterested in personal welfare
3. Over emphasis on "administravia"

---

1. Performance appraisal is not perceived helpful to improving work

"Rx" Recommendations and Remedies

Perception of District Administration

1. Hold more frequent staff forums
2. Encourage district administrators to conduct "consumer evaluations" and to act on the results
3. Identify staff "opinion leaders" and develop an internal key communicator's network
4. Increase visibility in buildings

Community Relations

1. Expand community education outreach to nonparents
2. Include nonparents on advisory committees, task forces, etc.
3. Use cable TV channel 22 to inform community of school activities/affairs
4. Find ways to recognize contributions of nonparents
5. Invite local civic clubs to hold one meeting a year in a local school
6. Invite senior citizens to sample school lunch
7. Open school libraries to the public
8. Expand Adults-in-high-school courses program
9. Continue sending one issue of the *ECHO* to all residents

Growth Opportunities

1. Encourage more assertive leadership by principals and supervisors in focusing "job targets" on improvement
2. Emphasize "consumer evaluation" at all levels
3. Expand staff input in developing inservice programs
4. Utilize results of the 1979-80 Inservice Needs Assessment to develop future programs
5. Activate SD^2 Committee
6. Consider building inservice programs (e.g. $4.000 would provide $500 for each building to conduct relevant inservice programs)
7. Consider individualized staff development programs
8 Find ways (other than salary increments) to recognize self-improvements

Interpersonal Relationships with Administrators

1. Emphasize the need for principals and supervisors to use "job target conferences" to recognize good performance
2. Encourage all administrators/supervisors to use "recognition notes" and congratulatory letters to deserving staff members
3. Expand School Board recognition of staff performance
4. Provide administrators inservice training on humanizing management
5. Review administrative procedures, reporting requirements, etc. in order to minimize bureaucracy

Supervisory Relationships

See Growth Opportunities Recommendations.

Figure 4–2 *(continued)*

MORALE MODEL

Positive morale is exemplified by staff members who:

- Are fresh every morning
- Care about the school and its image
- Tackle assigned tasks willingly
- Support the school's goals
- Actively promote and participate in school affairs and functions
- Exercise initiative in improving school–community relations
- Express pride in being part of the school
- Occasionally make second-mile efforts in behalf of the school, its program, and its students.

Figure 4–3

BUILDING BLOCKS FOR BETTER MORALE

Incentive Concerns	Contractual Concerns
• Achievement	• Salary
• Recognition	• Benefits
• Advancement	• Security
• Responsibility	• Working conditions
• Input	• Policies

Professional Concerns	Social Concerns
• Adequate materials	• Social affairs (luncheons, banquets, picnics)
• Flexible curriculum	• Retreats
• Planning time	• Bowling leagues, volleyball teams, and so on
• Opportunities for growth	• Nights out (ball games, concerts)
• Academic freedom	• Mixers
• Fair evaluation	

Figure 4–4

Provisions for the *contractual concerns* of the staff are most often hammered out at the bargaining table through the negotiations process. Chapter 2 itemized specific means for successfully addressing these concerns in order to satisfy staff needs and demands, while at the same time contributing to the overall goals of the system.

Professional concerns relate to the ease with which and extent to which staff members are provided the time and tools necessary to accomplish assigned tasks and stated goals. Effective school leaders realize that reasonable efforts must be made to accommodate these needs in the interest of overall high morale and positive progress of the school program.

Not all employees want their work place and their coworkers to serve as the center of their social life. Nevertheless, all faculties and employee groups are social institutions. Working relationships are expanded and enhanced when they are supported by positive social relationships. Where staff morale, camaraderie, and performance are highest, specific steps have been taken to meet the *social concerns* of all members of the group.

In short, all of these building blocks are fundamental to promoting and preserving a healthy and productive climate for all staff members.

Much of the burden for focusing on the four primary areas of morale concern described above is borne by the building administrator. The principal has the most direct access to the most manageable-sized group of certified and classified staff members within the school framework. His or her leadership is largely responsible for the tone of the school.

COMMON PERSONNEL PITFALLS FOR PRINCIPALS

Unfortunately, the pressures of immediate management and crisis control prevent some principals from directing enough skill and attention to the more important building blocks for better morale. This section pinpoints some of the most common mistakes that entrap building leaders and hamper successful morale management within the school.

The principal serves as the key actor in positive personnel management and morale maintenance within any school. His or her behavior in establishing interpersonal relationships serves as a model for the way other staff members treat one another and, more importantly, how they relate to children and parents. Principals must utilize social skills to promote staff unity and avoid faculty alienation. Albert Schweitzer once commented, "Example is not the *main* thing in influencing others. It is the *only* thing." This axiom should serve as an overriding principle for personnel practices on the part of all administrators. Staffs are ordinarily incapable of growing beyond the capability of the principal.

Too often, however, morale sags and personnel management is impaired because principals (and other school leaders) fall prey to seemingly inconsequential attitudes, behaviors, habits, and practices that negate other efforts to promote harmony among staff members. Many of the personnel pitfalls that jeopardize building-level morale seem trivial and represent patterns that are easily acquired. Their cumulative impact, nevertheless, can be devastating to the general interpersonal climate within the school.

The following are some of the most common failings that foster disharmony and poor human relations in the school:

- Avoidance behavior (a consuming concern for escaping criticism, controversy, unpopular positions, and so on)
- Failure to see and treat all employees as individuals capable of growth and change
- Overemphasis on administrative mystique (distance, aloofness, and so on)
- Reliance on impersonal solutions to people problems (mass instruction, group punishment, and so on)
- Exhibiting favoritism or cronyism
- Demonstrating paternalism
- Playing politics
- Projecting a false sense of ownership ("my school," "my kids," and so on)
- Double dealing, working both sides of the street
- Permitting the principal's personal life to invade and intrude on school life
- Categorizing, labeling, or stereotyping segments of the staff or student body (minority groups, older teachers, and so on)
- Viewing all problems as signs of weakness on the part of the staff
- A fixation with fixing blame
- Overconcern with a Good Guy image (compulsion to please everyone)
- Limiting praise and lavishing criticism
- Modeling bigotry
- Courting parent favor
- Providing unclear or unrealistic expectations and directions
- Rationalizing personal weaknesses
- Adopting a closed door policy
- Exhibiting inconsistency
- Practicing disloyalty
- Putting people on hold, literally and figuratively
- Evidencing rivalry or jealousy with other principals or administrators
- Belittling, ridiculing, or criticizing individuals in the presence of others
- Protracting meetings unnecessarily
- Embracing ambiguity, a tendency to be vague
- Expressing contempt for subordinates not present
- Obsession with trivia

In addition to avoiding the pitfalls identified above, the morale-conscious administrator should develop an action plan designed to eliminate or alleviate the major factors that undermine staff performance. To the extent that these negative forces can be diminished, staff morale will improve proportionally. The next section spells out the primary inhibitors of maximum staff productivity.

TEN OBSTACLES TO POSITIVE STAFF PERFORMANCE

Morale can only soar where the possibility of achieving desired outcomes is real and recognized. One fundamental function of positive personnel management is to make the working (teaching, learning) environment as rich and unfettered as possible. To accomplish this end, principals and other school officials must understand those roadblocks which most commonly limit the staff's chances for success.

Outlined in Figure 4–5 are ten of the most common obstacles to high staff performance. These deterrents often serve as a starting point for improving both working conditions and staff attitudes. If the principal can clear away all or most of these obstructions, pathways to better performance and increased satisfaction will be opened up significantly.

Based on the information outlined above, any administrator can build a program to make the school setting a work place charged with positive interpersonal relationships, mutual support, and employee excitement.

HINTS ON BOOSTING MORALE AT THE BUILDING LEVEL

In school systems, as elsewhere, most important problems are solved in the front-line trenches. Even though favorable staff relations, satisfactory communication channels, and positive vibes may exist at the district level, it is the state of morale within the building unit that ultimately makes or breaks the system's efforts to ensure maximum staff performance and goal attainment. Obviously, the principal serves as the primary catalyst in determining the positive or negative valence of staff unity in the building-level work force.

Principals are called upon to carry out myriad functions—some monumental, some mundane. In a world of changing roles and revised job descriptions, it is sometimes difficult for principals themselves to perceive clearly what their real responsibilities are and what their priorities should be.

As a tongue-in-cheek illustration of the building leader's multifaceted function, the students at one elementary school were asked to answer the question, "What does a principal do?" The responses, in Figure 4–6, illustrate the role confusion that stalks many modern elementary and secondary principals.

In addition to the chores identified in that pupil poll, perhaps the number one item on most successful principals' job agendas is nurturing a positive team climate and a collegial atmosphere among the entire building staff.

The first step in that process is for the principal to exert second-mile efforts to demand and expect the best from every staff member and to serve as a model in

TEN OBSTACLES TO POSITIVE STAFF PERFORMANCE

1. Overload of nonteaching chores (paperwork, "reportomania," and so on)
2. A rigid hierarchy and inflexible scheduling, which dictate programs and limit personal style and autonomy
3. Administrative dominance and interference
4. Low staff self-esteem (high self-concept is no longer an automatic accompaniment to a teaching career)
5. Substandard working conditions (large class size, incidents of violence and vandalism, inadequate materials, tacky surroundings, and so on)
6. Lack of direction, communication, support, and input opportunities from supervisors
7. Inconsistent policies and wavering disposition on the part of leaders
8. Public criticism and lack of appreciation (evidenced by uncaring, uninvolved parents)
9. Lack of personal goal setting by teachers and administrators
10. Boredom and burnout

Figure 4–5

WHAT DOES A PRINCIPAL DO?

Reprinted from the October 1980 issue of <u>Know Your Schools</u>, St. Louis Park, Minnesota.

"The principal is the owner of the school."

"He tells the children to go home."

"If you're lost he shows you the way."

"He talks to bad kids and asks them why they did it."

"He makes the school tidy and stops fights."

"He does very hard work and he works hard at it."

"He makes sure no one climbs up on the walls."

Figure 4—6

working with people. Further aids to the principal that have proved successful for bolstering building-level morale are in the following checklist:

- ☑ Use faculty meetings and individual conferences to create an accepting atmosphere that makes change possible.
- ☑ Share decision making. Teachers show more enthusiasm when allowed to participate regularly and actively.
- ☑ Establish standard operating procedures for processing parent complaints.
- ☑ Evidence concern about the quality of the teachers' work place.
- ☑ Protect teachers from unscheduled interruptions (sales representatives, solicitors, and sometimes even central office supervisors).
- ☑ Provide privacy (particularly telephone privacy) wherever possible.
- ☑ Take special pains with beginners (buddy systems, survival kits, and so on).
- ☑ Make every effort to understand and accommodate the unique faculty culture within the building.
- ☑ Seek ways for the staff to share individual and mutual joy and pain.
- ☑ Provide time for advisement.
- ☑ Demonstrate acts of encouragement wherever possible.
- ☑ Get to know the real interests of the staff through use of a concern profile (staff submission of unsigned questions that concern them most).
- ☑ Rotate leadership responsibilities and assignments.
- ☑ Maintain and radiate a positive view of youth.
- ☑ Develop a position description for teachers which provides a professional, nonproduction-line challenge (see sample in Figure 4–7).
- ☑ Support teachers in conflict situations.
- ☑ Assign regular and extra duties on an impartial basis.
- ☑ Actively do things with others for others, but not to others.
- ☑ Remember itinerant staff members and traveling teachers (see Figure 4–8, Morale Reminders for Itinerant Personnel).
- ☑ Welcome subordinates as both contributors and critics.
- ☑ Conduct exit interviews for staff members leaving the building in order to learn areas of satisfaction and discontent.
- ☑ Avoid hip-pocket decisions that disregard staff feelings and concerns.
- ☑ Provide opportunities for observation of other teachers, visitations to other levels, exchange teaching, and so on.
- ☑ Make every effort to match abilities and interests to assigned duties.
- ☑ Actively protect the teacher's right to improvise.
- ☑ Remember that periodic pep talks can work miracles in rekindling enthusiasm and unity.

ELEMENTARY OR SECONDARY TEACHER JOB DESCRIPTION

Responsibilities

1. Planning, organizing, and providing appropriate learning experiences within assigned areas of responsibility.
2. Establishing and maintaining a classroom atmosphere conducive to learning.
3. Evaluating and interpreting student learning in a professional manner.
4. Identifying special needs of students and seeking assistance as needed.
5. Making reasonable efforts to promote and maintain appropriate behavior of students.
6. Contributing to the continuous development of curriculum and the improvement of instruction.
7. Maintaining records and submitting necessary reports for the effective management of the school program.
8. Participating in faculty meetings, workshops, in-service training, and other appropriate activities.
9. Adhering to ethical standards adopted by professional teacher organizations.

Figure 4–7

MORALE REMINDERS FOR ITINERANT PERSONNEL

1. Pay special attention to itinerant travelers and staff specialists who work in several buildings but are assigned to none (the educational nomads of the district).

2. This segment of the staff often misses routine announcements, is overlooked in the distribution and routing of materials, and is unable to attend individual faculty meetings.

3. Such personnel often feel uninformed and outside the mainstream of building activities.

4. Contacts and communication with the itinerant staff can be strengthened through:

   • Monthly miscellany memos providing updates on building and district doings

   • Quarterly gatherings of itinerant personnel to fill in gaps and answer questions

   • Forwarding copies of all minutes, notices, and so on

Figure 4–8

EMERGENCY ALERT TEAM

An Emergency Alert Team has been organized at the Senior High School. The purpose of the team is to assist with medical-type emergencies that may occur in the classroom or other areas of the school building.

Examples of these emergencies include epileptic seizure, heart attack, choking, unconsciousness, broken bones, dislocations, overdose of drugs, and so on. If you are in need of assistance for such an emergency, please dial 550 on your red phone, tell the person answering, "Blue alert," and give the location of the emergency. The information will be announced and the team will come to assist you as soon as possible.

Figure 4–9

☑ Establish a building-level emergency alert team (see sample staff announcement in Figure 4–9).

☑ Increase availability by being in the outer office at the beginning and end of each staff work day. Make it a point to greet teachers every morning.

☑ Demonstrate a willingness to substitute for teachers, help on field trips, and assist aides whenever necessary.

☑ Make an extra effort to listen for the feelings behind the words during individual conferences.

☑ Provide immediate and specific feedback whenever appropriate.

☑ Supplement regular faculty meetings with smaller group sessions whenever necessary.

☑ Stage a faculty art show (see sample notice in Figure 4–10).

☑ Practice perception checking by validating impressions of staff positions through direct questioning, paraphrasing, and so on.

☑ Stress the importance of positive lounge talk.

☑ Place a high priority on challenging and exciting building and individual goals each year.

☑ Substitute face-to-face contacts for written memos and directions whenever possible.

LITTLE MORALE MEASURES THAT MAKE A BIG DIFFERENCE

In addition to following the kinds of general strategies suggested above, continued high morale at both the building and district level is often best sustained by a multitude of down-to-earth, mini-measures that are within the reach of every administrator.

Although comprehensive programs of morale improvement are necessary and effective, staff perceptions and attitudes are often influenced more by modest, quiet gestures of administrative concern and respect. The following low-cost, high-return morale boosters can be implemented effectively in any school situations:

- Establish a "no solicitation" rule.
- Give staff first crack at surplus sales items.
- Respect the intercom.
- Provide plug-in heaters and car-starting service in cold climates.
- Offer retirement and estate-planning programs for staff members.
- Provide reserved parking.
- Include spouses in workshops, special events, and so on.
- Remember birthdays.
- Send clips of articles to staff members recognized in print.
- Permit staff to ride school buses without charge.

the Gallery
Eliot Center
6800 Cedar Lake Rd   St Louis Pk, Mn

FACULTY ART SHOW

artists employed by School District 283

OPENING:

FRIDAY, NOVEMBER 21, 1980
6 to 9 pm

Refreshments and Conversation

GALLERY HOURS: Tues & Thurs 5-8 PM

Show continues through December 5

PARTICIPATING ARTISTS

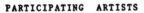

Bob Anderson
Ardelle Athmann
Myra Damm
Charles Deckas
Doris Engel
Donna Getsinger
Karen Hansen
Elaine Hautman
Florence Hill
Ranny Mittendorff
Opal Oleson
Eleanor Olson
Evelyn Pius
Sandy Stokes
Sarah Zeug

Figure 4-10

Certificate of Appreciation

Presented to

Whose interest, enthusiasm and effort has resulted in outstanding achievement. We are proud that you are a part of the St. Louis Park School District.

School Board Chairperson

Superintendent of Schools

Figure 4–11

- Provide lighted parking lots and safe escorts to cars at night.
- Host annual banquets to honor retirees and recognize years of service.
- Issue T–K (Teachers' Kid) passes to athletic events.

- Keep surroundings pleasant (new paint, no ratty furniture, and so on).
- Permit early departure on Fridays.
- Send condolences.
- Establish a staff Professional Leave Committee.
- Provide incentives for innovation through ICP (innovative classroom practices) mini-grants.

- Offer consumer services to employees.
- Issue certificates of appreciation (see sample form in Figure 4–11).

- Permit staff to enroll in community education classes free of charge.
- Round up a collection of small gifts for teachers at the start of each year.
- Provide a notary public on staff.
- Provide a staff ombudsman.
- Issue "Thanks for Being a Pro" notes.
- Allow some choice in determining individual reporting and departure times where possible.

KEYS TO IMPROVED STAFF COMMUNICATION

The underlying theme common to most morale improvement efforts is simply open, active, two-way communication. This section contains a variety of practical techniques for increasing staff communication and interaction, which can be adopted at all levels.

One primary premise of positive personnel management is that a better-informed employee is an asset to the entire school operation. The 12 action suggestions below can be employed by any administrator and will go a long way in establishing a free-and-easy, give-and-take atmosphere.

As initial steps in improving staff communication, many schools have found it beneficial to try one or more of the following strategies:

1. Provide specific written feedback to written lesson plans where they are required.
2. Provide printed agendas in advance for all meetings.
3. Establish a Superintendents Advisory Council (see sample bylaws in Figure 4–12).
4. Conduct periodic Staff Forums in which any employee can voice concerns, complaints, and commendations directly to the school board.
5. Establish School Advisory Councils (see sample guidelines in Figure 4 –13).

6. Provide periodic informal presentations (viewpoints) from the superintendent directly to the staff and community via cable TV.

7. Where faculties are large, develop a Faculty Senate or School Cabinet.

8. Hold weekly preschool breakfasts for interested staff members.

9. Issue weekly bulletins from the principal designed to highlight goals, feature accomplishments, make announcements, and outline forthcoming events.

10. Place suggestion boxes in each building so that all staff members can submit agenda items for the School Cabinet, Superintendent's Advisory Council, faculty meetings, and so on.

11. Hold regular meetings with all department heads.

12. Issue a regular, districtwide staff letter, preferably following each school board meeting (see sample in Figure 4–14).

One caution that should be considered in activating the morale measures suggested throughout this chapter is that most of them apply to all employees within the building, not just faculty members.

POINTERS FOR PAYING SPECIAL ATTENTION TO SUPPORT PERSONNEL

The needs for a feeling of connectedness with the school, positive peer support, self-esteem, and high morale are not limited to teaching personnel only. Every employee (secretaries, custodians, food service staff, and so on) deserves respect, recognition, and treatment as a worthy individual and important contributor to the school's operation.

Too often, however, support personnel are left out of the mainstream of decision making, ignored in administration's efforts to improve morale, and gain a sense of second-class citizenship within the school.

An effective program of positive personnel management must relate directly to the total staff. Consequently, it behooves school managers to pay special attention to the nonteaching—but not nonessential—members of the school team in order to maximize productivity and performance of the entire staff.

The pointers below illustrate tangible tactics that can be employed to heighten morale among support personnel:

- Include support personnel in all social events, treat lists, planning, committies, decision making, birthday celebrations, routings, recognition, staff meetings, mailings, staff development, office arrangements.

- Develop workshops specifically designed to meet the needs of the support staff.

- Provide support personnel with survival kits of key information (maps, calendars, bus schedules, phone numbers, and so on).

- Encourage growth on the part of all support staff members (membership in Professional Secretaries International, and so on).
- Include events affecting classified personnel on school calendars.
- Identify the opinion leaders in the support personnel ranks and utilize these individuals as key communicators within the staff.
- Consider establishing a Classified Employees Council.
- Host secretary luncheons, cookouts, custodians' barbecues, and so on.
- Arrange offices so that people are placed by personal temperature preferences as much as possible.
- Accommodate the needs of both smokers and nonsmokers.
- Consider occasionally shortening the lunch hour and releasing clerical personnel early.

By following the morale improvement measures provided throughout this chapter, administrators can make significant strides in achieving high productivity and satisfaction from all of the human resources in the school.

SUPERINTENDENT'S ADVISORY COUNCIL BYLAWS

Purpose

The purpose of the organization shall be to further communication and interaction between the total professional staff and the superintendent and the administrative team. The role of the council shall be to raise questions, react to ideas, and make suggestions and recommendations. In this way, the membership can help map the direction of the school system.

Membership

Except as provided in the third paragraph under "Term of Membership," the council shall consist of one staff member from each elementary school, one staff member from each junior high school, two senior high staff members, one person representing staff specialists and the Department of Pupil Services, and one administrator.

Term of Membership

The term of membership shall be two years. No member shall serve more than one term, except that a council member shall be eligible for election to a full term if the member has served no more than one year of an unexpired term.

Terms shall be staggered so that half of the membership is selected each year.

Any member who loses his or her constituency because of displacement shall be allowed to complete the term of membership.

Elections

Elections shall be held annually by September 15. Those elected shall assume their positions at the beginning of the following year.

Current members shall assume responsibility for the election procedure for their respective categories.

In the event of a vacancy, the group respresented shall select a person to serve the remainder of the unexpired term.

Figure 4—12

Meetings

Regular monthly meetings and special meetings as needed shall be held under the chairmanship of the superintendent. All meetings shall be scheduled at 3:15 P.M., unless otherwise determined. Released time will be provided as necessary for members to attend meetings.

The agenda shall be determined in advance by the membership, but members may present other items for consideration. There is no restriction on the potential subject matter for consideration by the council, as long as it has to do with improving the educational program or school system in general. However, matters deemed inappropriate, after being heard, shall be referred to the proper office or agency.

The manner of keeping and distributing records of council proceedings shall be determined by the council.

Disposition of Council Recommendations

All decisions and recommendations of the council shall be considered by the superintendent for action. The superintendent shall keep the members informed of pursuant action taken.

Figure 4–12 *(continued)*

ADVISORY COUNCIL GUIDELINES

TO: School Board Members, Executive Committee, and Elementary
           Principals
FROM: Mike Smith
SUBJECT: Guidelines for Formation of Elementary School Advisory Councils

One of the major elements of the elementary reorganization beginning in the forthcoming school year will be the formation of an advisory council to serve each of the four elementary schools. The intent of the advisory council concept is to provide a new role for parents and staff in advising the building principals regarding all major aspects of the elementary program as it operates in each of the buildings. Because each building principal is responsible for the operation of his or her respective building, it seems desirable to establish a separate advisory council to work with each of the principals, with the understanding that the advisory groups for paired schools will meet together on occasion in order to focus on elements related to integration of the two school programs and the two respective school communities.

However, because of the fact that many details regarding next year, including assignments of staff, have yet to be worked out, forming such councils permanently at this time does not seem either wise or feasible. In the interim, then, it seems desirable for the principal responsible for each of next year's four remaining elementary buildings to form an ad hoc advisory group for that building as soon as possible to serve as a focal point for community concerns and communication during this transition period. The ad hoc group will serve in an advisory capacity during this time and will eventually be replaced early next fall with the more permanent community–school advisory council.

Some of the activities these groups could address in the interim could include the following:

1. Identifying and recommending possible solutions to community concerns regarding next year's reorganization.
2. Assisting in providing an orderly transition for children and parents.
3. Providing a communications link for transition activities in the school's attendance area.
4. Providing information regarding community concerns to the staff transition committee.
5. Assisting in the planning of activities to help acquaint new parents and students with their schools and to help establish a bond between the paired school communities.
6. Beginning some of the preliminary discussions about the structure and development of the permanent advisory council to be formed in the early fall.

Figure 4–13

7. Discussing the role and relationship of the advisory councils to the respective PTSA units that now exist in each of the buildings, since these units are the only formally existing parent–school advisory group that focuses on the entire school program.

8. Providing a forum for participation of preschool parents in community–school activities and programs.

Membership

Because of the uncertainty of staff assignments, it is my feeling that the membership of these particular committees should consist of any community person residing in the attendance area that will be served by the particular school, or who will have children attending the particular school, regardless of whether that individual currently has children in school. The most important criterion is an interest in the elementary program and a willingness to work for its successful implementation. If the level of interest and participation at a given building is exceptionally high the group can organize itself so that it can work more effectively (by use of an executive committee, subcommittees, and so on).

Advisory Nature

It is important to note that the nature of these groups is that of an advisory body, and the final responsibility for decision making remains with the principal, the district administration, and the school board. However, the concerns and advice of the group will receive full and serious consideration in any decision that is made.

Principals' Role and Relationship

It is important that the principals of each of the four elementary buildings serve as the focal points for these transition committees. It would also seem advisable to involve the current PTA leadership as well as other interested and committed community members. Staff members who wish to attend or participate would also be welcome, although the absence of staff assignments for next year may be a factor limiting this participation. When the permanent advisory councils are formed next year, the role of those councils will be to advise the principals directly on all aspects of school operation and to serve as a sounding board and communications link with the broader community. These councils will then consist of both staff and community members on a limited, representative basis. The principals can serve an important role at this early point by setting high standards for open communication, a broad perspective, and recognition of the important contributions community members make to the educational process. The four elementary principals for next year should now proceed to establish an initial organizational meeting for the ad hoc group. It is my hope that the organizational process will not preoccupy the group, since its ad hoc nature and relatively short time frame would not seem to allow for spending much time with such concerns. The initial agenda is probably suggested by the list of concerns at the beginning of this memo; however, you are free to structure the meeting, and the agenda, in any way you see fit. If you have any questions, please contact me.

Figure 4–13 *(continued)*

STAFFLETTER

School Board Highlights

The St. Louis Park School Board held its regular March 22, 1982 meeting at 8:00 p.m. in the Senior High Board Room.

FACILITY USE
RECOMMENDATION

The Board voted to consider the sale and lease of both Ethel Baston and Fern Hill. This enables the Board to maintain the broadest number of options in the disposition of the buildings. Dr. Hickey said that it does not appear that holding on to one of the buildings as a hedge against increased enrollment will be necessary. He said while projections show a slight upward trend by the mid-eighties, the remaining facilities seem adequate. In a real pinch, he added, the school district could re-open one of the schools currently used as a community center.

1982-83 INTERIM
GIFTED PROGRAM

The Board approved a recommendation to reorganize the district's Gifted and Talented program in the light of budget reductions. The recommendation included the following elements:

K-6	1.5 FTE
7-12	1.0 FTE
Secretary	.5 FTE

The plan eliminates district-wide coordination of the program for one year. Dr. Hickey noted that specialized leadership in this area is necessary and its absence is on an interim basis only. Dr. Hickey said the plan is designed to give reasonably balanced, direct services to students across the K-12 program.

ELEMENTARY
ATTENDANCE BOUNDARIES

The Board approved 1982-83 elementary attendance boundaries. Copies of the boundaries will be sent to each school for distribution.

JUNIOR HIGH ATHLETIC
PROGRAM

The Board approved a Junior High athletic program for 1982-83. The program, which includes football, volleyball, cross country, basketball, swimming, track and support personnel will cost $27,100. The Junior High PTSA will pick up $4,000 of the cost leaving the School Board with an actual cost of $23,100. The program eliminates tennis, gymnastics, and synchronized swimming and makes soccer an intramural activity. It also provides equal sports opportunities for boys and girls.

Figure 4-14 *(continued)*

SECONDARY 1-2 MILE TRANSPORTATION	The Board approved a local discretionary levy to raise .05 mill in order to provide bus transportation for senior high students living between one and two miles from the Senior High.
POLICY ON DISTRIBUTION OF MATERIALS TO SCHOOLS	The Board voted to reaffirm the current policy concerning the distribution of announcements and other information to the schools.
BUSINESS AGENDA	In the business agenda the Board: 1) passed a resolution authorizing the May 18 School Board election; 2) set an hourly rate of $3.35 for election judges and an hourly rate of $3.75 for chairpersons and counting center judges; 3) approved investments; 4) approved bills and payroll; 5) approved electronic fund transfers; 6) set May 19 at 4:00 p.m. as a special meeting time to canvass the vote of the Board Election, May 18.

INFORMATION ON LIFE LICENSES AVAILABLE

On March 30, 1982, the rule governing the issuance of life licenses which was adopted by the Minnesota Board of Teaching will become effective. Completed life license applications will be accepted by the Personnel Licensing Section of the State Department of Education until July 1, 1982.

Each school will receive a copy of the procedures for the Issuance of Life Licenses and instruction for making application for a life license. The information will be posted at your school.

THE BEGINNING OF A REVOLUTION

Is there more talk than action on computer technology in the classroom? This is quite possible. With only 52,000 computers in classrooms in the country's 16,000 school districts, there are, on the average, only 3.2 computers available to students in each district.

According to a survey by the National Center for Education Statistics (NCES), one-half of the nation's secondary schools have at least one microcomputer or computer terminal, while only 14% of elementary schools and 19% of all other types of schools such as vocational or special education have the equipment.

Although many districts are talking about computer use, many also said their plans are uncertain. Only about 18% of the districts without computers plan to initiate computer use within three years, according to the NCES study.

Only one state, Minnesota, is considered greatly involved. In a survey by Electronic Learning magazine, only seven other states were listed as leading contributors to the development of computer education. Those states were Alaska, California, Delaware, Florida, North Carolina, Texas and Pennsylvania.

Educators are concerned about the new technological education. But despite the uncertainties of use, there is consensus—computers are on the way and predictions that within 10 years, "computers and videodiscs will provide a form of educational experience...superior to the textbook-dominated experience."

Reprinted by permission from EDUCATION U.S.A., Copyright 1982
National School Public Relations Association.

Figure 4-14 (continued)

CHAPTER SUPPLEMENTS

The following chapter supplements are included to illustrate the principles outlined in this chapter.

Contents:

- Criteria for Constructive Criticism
- Ways to Recognize Doers

CRITERIA FOR CONSTRUCTIVE CRITICISM

Although criticism can never be completely eliminated from the supervisor–employee relationship, the manner in which identification of weakness and suggestions for improvement are conveyed can have a major impact on individual and total staff morale and can largely determine whether or not the criticism produces desired results. The criteria below underscore ways to minimize the counterproductive effect of destructive criticism and to maximize the positive potential of constructive criticism:

- Avoid making criticism personal.
- Focus on behavior (or lack of it), rather than personality.
- Criticize in private.
- Avoid criticizing when angry.
- Base criticism on facts, not impression or rumors.
- Stress positive behaviors as well as weakness—build on strengths.
- Praise improvement.
- Convey support and a willingness to assist in the improvement process.
- Limit written criticism to essentials.
- Return or destroy letters or memorandam of criticism if permanent improvement ensues.

HOW TO RECOGNIZE DOERS

Chernow and Chernow* have identified the following checkpoints for locating the teachers or others on any staff who are the movers and shakers and, as trend setters, can become key allies in forming positive relations and cooperative team efforts within the schools:

- Measure output, not noise. It could be a mistake to classify automatically a silent teacher or assistant as a daydreamer. He or she may be quiet because he or she is busy.

- Beware of the assistant who claims to be a whiz at delegating. He or she may merely be an expert at avoiding work.

- A doer won't run from details. Don't be unduly impressed with the person who says he or she will handle the total picture and let others handle the details.

- Be suspicious of assistants who are always writing, telephoning, and dashing from one place to another. Don't assume they are doers. They may just be running away from a process that terrifies them—thinking.

- Don't pin too many hopes on the aide who wants to hold group meetings at the slightest provocation. The greater the do-it-yourself urge, the fewer the meetings.

- Some managers develop preconceived notions about what a doer looks like. Whether an individual is tall or short, stocky or slender, blond or bald, won't make the least bit of difference. Doers come in all shapes and sizes.

---

*Fred Chernow and Carol Chernow, *School Administrator's Guide to Managing People*, West Nyack, N.Y.: Parker Publishing Company, Inc., 1976, p. 163.

5

Down-to-Earth Tips for Improving the Ineffective Teacher

Despite the level of morale or teamwork evident within the staff, every school suffers from the presence of one or more marginal teachers whose perfunctory performance and mediocre productivity reduce the overall effectiveness of the total organization. Unfortunately, some of the simplistic solutions available in the private sector (such as summary and rapid dismissal) are not always easily applicable in a public institution. Strict tenure and due process laws in many states make teacher dismissal on grounds of incompetence or ineffectiveness a complicated and protracted process, sometimes spanning several years.

In most cases, practical administrators recognize the reality of having to retain and deal with a certain number of low-performance teachers on the job each year.

Improving the ineffective teacher constitutes a formidable challenge to the instructional leadership and personnel management skills of any school leader. Changing teacher behavior is delicate, difficult, and time-consuming. Usually, there is little assistance available to the administrator from the negotiated agreement or from the local teachers' association. Nevertheless, most teachers can be helped to achieve at least a satisfactory level of performance in the classroom. The primary tools required in this task are empathy, patience, a working knowledge of what makes good teaching, and high-level communication skills.

The remainder of this chapter details a variety of strategies for aiding sub-par performers to grow toward successful teaching and, in fact, for assisting all teachers to enhance their effectiveness in the classroom. The first condition for such improvement is a sound program of performance appraisal. A workable blueprint for this kind of program is outlined in the following section.

USING A JOB TARGET APPROACH TO STAFF IMPROVEMENT

Out of the countless schemes for teacher evaluation that have been concocted by school boards, administrators, college professors, and others down through the years, a few salient principles have emerged to make up the foundation of a performance appraisal program that really can improve instruction, salvage poor performers in the classroom, and make good teachers even better.

The ten-point plan for performance appraisal below pinpoints the necessary ingredients for a successful teacher evaluation procedure:

1. Teacher input and involvement in designing the program
2. A primary focus on improving instruction (not on fault finding, personal criticism, punitive measures, or possible dismissal)
3. Shared responsibility (evaluator and evaluatee) for identifying areas to be improved, appropriate growth opportunities, and resources required to effect change
4. A commitment to build on existing strengths
5. Prescribed limitations that make improvement a manageable task
6. Simplicity of process and procedure
7. Built-in provisions for monitoring progress and changing course when necessary
8. Periodic provision for teacher–administrator review and dialogue
9. Requirement for specific indicators of progress or lack of it
10. Recognition that not all goals are met and not all plans work (right to fail)

Derived from these ten basic tenets for successful evaluation, many school districts have adopted a job target approach to performance appraisal, which meets all of the stated criteria and has demonstrated measurable results in improving teacher effectiveness. The sample appraisal plan in Figure 5–1, job target form in Figure 5–2, and the sample appraisal figure in Figure 5–3 have worked in one suburban school district since 1977.

IMMEDIATE MEASURES FOR SOLVING
TEACHERS' DISCIPLINE PROBLEMS

Where a job target approach has been used, one of the most frequent areas targeted for improvement is discipline. In a vast number of cases, administrators have found that the chief cause of teacher ineffectiveness is lack of classroom control. When discipline is improved, overall teaching and learning effectiveness often rises accordingly. Thus, the first measure in helping many ineffective teachers to become more successful is to assist them in achieving a positive climate in the classroom.

GUIDELINES FOR APPRAISAL
OF TEACHER PROFESSIONAL PERFORMANCE

Background and Introduction

Following a three-year meet-and-confer committee study of teacher evaluation procedures, a new process and a new instrument for appraising professional performance was implemented according to the guidelines outlined below.

Statement of Purpose

The purposes of the professional appraisal plan are to improve instruction, provide accountability, and maximize teacher growth. The process features an atmosphere of mutual respect and responsibility. The plan is designed to bring teacher and evaluator together in a constructive partnership to assess job responsibilities and progress toward mutually determined job targets in an objective, positive, and purposeful fashion. It is intended that this partnership be characterized by open communication between the parties involved, taking into account the unique circumstances of each individual teaching situation.

General Instructions

- Every teacher will receive a formal evaluation in accordance with these guidelines, at least every two years. Such evaluations may occur more often if desired by either the appraiser or the appraisee.
- All probationary teachers and others in need of special assistance will be evaluated annually.
- At the beginning of the school year, each principal shall submit to the director of personnel a list of full and part-time teachers to be evaluated during each of the first two years of the program. Each year thereafter, the personnel office will generate and distribute a list of teachers scheduled for formal appraisal.
- Both teachers and evaluators may propose job targets intended to meet the needs of the students, the school, and the individual teacher. All job

Figure 5–1

targets are subject to the final approval of the principal, assistant principal, or other appropriate supervisor.

- Teachers not involved in the formal evaluation process in any given year will be required to submit to the building principal one or more carefully developed job targets. A self-evaluation report concerning the targets will also be submitted to the principal at the conclusion of the school year. Staff members are encouraged to use peer and student evaluations as sources of appraising progress toward target attainment.

- The responsibility for evaluating itinerant personnel will be determined by the administrative cabinet.

- This appraisal program will be reviewed at the end of the first two-year cycle.

Suggested Timetable

The following appraisal calendar should be followed in implementing the appraisal program (during the initial year, some adjustments will be necessary):

May 15	– September 15	Teacher submits proposed job targets.
September 15	– October 15	Evaluator schedules individual conferences to finalize job targets and review job responsibilities.
October 15	– March 31	Meetings held as necessary to review progress toward job targets.
April 1	– April 30	Teacher completes self-appraisal and submits forms to evaluator.
May 1	– June 5	Final appraisal conference is conducted. Review by a third party may be requested. All appraisals are completed and a copy filed in the personnel office.

Questions concerning this appraisal program may be directed to the director of personnel.

Figure 5–1 (continued)

APPRAISAL OF PROFESSIONAL PERFORMANCE

NAME _____ SCHOOL _____ POSITION _____

   1. Failed to meet job target (requires comments)
   2. Partially completed job target (requires comments)
   3. Completed job target (include comments for commendable accomplishment)

   JOB TARGET

   Number_____

   Method of implementation:

   Method of evaluation:

Comments by appraiser

Comments by appraisee:

Figure 5–2

APPRAISAL OF PROFESSIONAL PERFORMANCE

<u>Other comments on general or related aspects of performance:</u>*

<u>Record of conferences (dates):</u>

Evaluator _____ Date _____

Teacher _____ Date _____

Signature indicates he or she has reviewed the appraisal and received a copy.

Review requested _____ Date _____

_____

*Appraisee may respond if he or she so desires.

Figure 5–3

Although discipline problems are common, sources of help for teachers and administrators are likewise plentiful. Because of the public's ongoing concern with discipline in the public schools, innumerable agencies, organizations, projects, and publications in recent years have been devoted to providing practical aid for better classroom control. As one example, the author's *Educator's Discipline Handbook* (West Nyack, N.Y.: Parker Publishing Company, Inc., 1981) offers a comprehensive collection of successful discipline techniques and practices that have worked in scores of schools from every corner of the country. A wide array of similar sources of assistance is available to every school staff.

When discipline is the cause of classroom ineffectiveness, the initial step for any school leader should be to become thoroughly familiar with the wide range of resources available and to make the proper connection between the teachers needing help and the resources that can provide assistance. In some cases, an individual reading program can generate significant personal improvement. In other situations, a systematic program of staff development (workshops, visitations, discussion groups, and so on) for individual teachers or for the entire staff is necessary. In any event, there is no excuse for administrators to fail to find help for teachers in improving discipline. Countless examples from schools of all sizes have shown that good disciplines is possible in any school and in any classroom.

From all of the myriad discipline plans and approaches developed over the past several decades, the following two overriding principles consistently loom up as the basis for sound classroom control and a positive atmosphere in the school:

1. A successful, holistic approach to discipline requires special attention to prevention and positive reinforcement as well as to rules and consequences.
2. Discipline is best where teachers and parents have worked together to design a simple plan that can be applied consistently throughout the entire school and receive widespread community support.

One way to apply the first principle in solving discipline-based ineffectiveness problems is to provide teachers with a workable list of reinforcers for rewarding positive behavior in the classroom. The list in Figure 5–4, compiled from the work of Madeline Hunter (UCLA Lab School) and a variety of other sources, has served many staffs in improving behavior by catching pupils being good.

In addition to applying the principle of positive reinforcement, many teachers can be helped with problems of classroom control and ineffectiveness by participating, along with other staff members, administrators, parents, and community representatives, in formulating a consistent schoolwide or districtwide discipline plan. An example of one such plan appears in Figure 5–5.

HINTS ON HELPING TEACHERS TO INDIVIDUALIZE INSTRUCTION

Besides helping teachers to improve discipline as described above, administrators and supervisors can often have immediate impact on strengthening classroom

A POTPOURRI OF POSITIVE CLASSROOM REINFORCERS

Reinforcers for Individual Pupils

- Opportunity to eat lunch with the teacher
- Released time to use the school's computer
- Free library time
- "Happy Grams" to parents
- Extra time in a favorite learning center
- First crack at a new book or manipulative materials
- Honor roll (for behavior)
- Special privileges
- Reassuring touches
- Reciprocal smiles
- Selection as teacher's assistant for the day
- Blue ribbon awards
- Tokens or candy
- Stickers or temporary tattoos
- Opportunity to run errands or perform fun chores
- Released time to tape record stories for other students
- Chance to be first in line
- Extra time to work in the nature center
- Selection as "Student of the Week"

Reinforcers for Groups of Students

- Appropriate verbal praise
- Special visits from the principal, school board members, local VIP's
- Classroom popcorn party
- Extra physical education or recess time
- Additional self-directed time
- Class sing-alongs
- Special field trips
- An extra edition of the class newsletter
- Shared time with other classes
- Comic book or paperback book exchanges
- Talent show
- Special games or contests
- Rereading aloud of a favorite story by the teacher
- Surprise party
- Class play or TV show
- Opportunity to bring pets to school
- Free passes to athletic events
- Recognition at an all-school assembly program

Figure 5–4

Elementary
Discipline
Plan

Dear Parent/Guardian:

This year all the elementary centers in St. Louis Park will share a district-wide discipline plan. This plan is the work of a committee of parents and staff members who agreed that a student discipline plan should have a positive emphasis while helping children to function properly in the school setting.

As a parent you play an important role in the success of this plan. We'd like you to read the philosophy, rules and consequences with your child. Then sign the form below, clip and return to your child's teacher. When staff, students and parents all know the rules and work together, our chances of maintaining a good school climate are greatly increased.

 Philosophy

The students of the St. Louis Park Schools are entitled to learn and develop in a setting which promotes respect of self, others, and property.

 Rules

Students will contribute to maintaining a school environment that promotes learning by:
- Using self-control and showing respect for fellow students, others, and property.
- Acting to insure the safety of everyone.
- Allowing orderly operation of the building.
- Accepting adult direction.
- Using appropriate language and actions.

Students that contribute to a positive environment will earn:
- Praise
- Notes and telephone calls home
- Rewards as determined by the classroom teacher

Figure 5–5

Consequences

First, Second, Third Consequence — Conference with observing/responsible adult. Appropriate action taken.

Fourth Consequence — "Time-Out," Principal notified.

Fifth Consequence — Letter form sent home signed by teacher and principal. Parent to return next day.

Sixth Consequence — Home/school conference with principal, involved staff and parents.

Seventh Consequence — In-house suspension (aide supervised).

Eighth Consequence — Suspension (½ day, 1 day) *Child Study Team meets with possible referrals for child and/or parent.

Ninth Consequence — Expulsion with school board approval.

Severe disruption or continual offense will result in moving directly to consequence seven and eight.

*Child Study Team may be involved at any time but must be at Consequence Eight.

Dear _____ :

We read and understand the Discipline Plan for our school;

| _____ | _____ |
| Student Signature | Parent/Guardian Signature |

| _____ | _____ |
| Date | Date |

Figure 5–5 *(continued)*

effectiveness by providing proven, practical means for teachers to individualize instruction for all students. This section highlights a number of action-oriented alternatives to the prevailing practice of lock-step, group-paced instruction.

Much of modern-day teaching effectiveness hinges on a high level of individualization (or personalization) of instruction. When skillful school personnel managers are concerned with improving ineffective teachers and helping all teachers to do their job better, one of the first places to concentrate is on promoting better ways to implement or enhance individualized approaches to teaching and learning.

Classroom excitement, teacher productivity, pupil progress, parental support, and the attainment of organizational goals are all heightened when teachers find meaningful methods of personalizing instruction and meeting the needs of students on an individual basis.

Just as school leaders frequently must deal with staff members one at a time in carrying out positive personnel practices in the school, effective teachers recognize that students learn only one at a time and teach accordingly.

In order to assist staff members to individualize instruction, it is important for principals and other leaders to understand that most efforts to tailor teaching to individual needs fall into one of the following four categories:

1. *Individual diagnosis and prescription*—The school identifies goals, materials, and methods of learning.
2. *Self-directed instruction*—The school sets goals. The student then identifies methods and materials.
3. *Personalized instruction*—The student selects goals. The school then prescribes methods and materials.
4. *Independent Study*—The student identifies goals, methods, and materials of learning.

Common Characteristics of Individualized Instruction

All of these general approaches share certain elements or adaptations of the common characteristics of individualized instruction outlined below:

- Some provision for individual assessment and self-paced instruction
- Individualized scheduling
- Personalized progress reporting
- Specific objectives (usually written) for individual pupils
- Availability of multilevel, multimedia materials to match student needs
- Student-directed movement
- Student participation in selection of goals, objectives, materials, and activities
- Personalized student–teacher planning
- Emphasis on student inquiry

Any of the four major approaches to individualization described above can be introduced successfully in schools and classrooms where the leadership is committed and the staff is open to change. The crucial factor for success is a genuine belief on the part of the individual teachers involved that the particular approach employed is workable and worthwhile.

In many situations, however, administrators have found that a low-key approach to expanding individualization of instruction is more palatable and productive than initiating any sweeping, full-blown new systems of education in the school.

Pathways to Personalizing Instruction

Where this is the case, the suggestions that follow can often open the door to aiding both effective and ineffective teachers in finding successful means to personalize the teaching–learning process without experiencing any sense of threat or intimidation:

1. Conduct voluntary building or districtwide workshops on practical methods of individualizing instruction. (Where possible, school board members should be included in these sessions.)

2. Expand the number of reading and math groups at each grade level by creating larger building units through "pairing"—establishment of primary (K–3) and intermediate (4–6) centers.

3. Introduce learning centers as a viable means of providing variegated learning experiences within the classroom.

4. Phase in a series of monthly or quarterly mini-courses or interim programs conducted by volunteers or staff members based on pupil interest and selection.

5. Pilot a controlled program of community-based education (CBE).

6. Develop alternative programs within the school or the district.

7. Explore provisions for alternative paths to graduation (evening classes, community service, internships for credit, and so on).

8. Adapt the rudiments (without the red tape) of federally mandated IEPs (individual educational plans) for special-education students by developing a simplified PEP (personalized educational plan) for all pupils.

9. Incorporate emerging technology (such as microcomputers, interactive cable TV, word processing centers), as a means of instructing and managing individualized learning.

Beyond the easy-to-implement tips for helping teachers to individualize instruction, additional assistance can be found, where appropriate, in a number of prepackaged programs and plans that can be made available to any staff. Among the most popular of these ready-made systems available for immediate implementation are the following:

Project PLAN (Program for Learning in Accordance with Needs), American Institute for Research, Palo Alto, California.

IPI (Individually Prescribed Instruction), Research for Better Schools, Inc., Philadelphia, Pennsylvania.

IGE (Individually Guided Education), Wisconsin Research and Development Center for Cognitive Learning, University of Wisconsin, Madison, Wisconsin.

PRACTICAL WAYS TO MATCH TEACHING AND LEARNING STYLES

An extra dimension is rapidly being added to the school's capacity to deal effectively with individual differences. As a plethora of research findings unfold providing new insights into how people learn, administrators and teachers are beginning to have an added handle on some of the causes of real and perceived teacher ineffectiveness with certain students.

In order to provide real help for teachers who evidence substandard performance in the classroom, it behooves all educational leaders to become aware of these research results and to understand the ramifications of these findings for bolstering classroom productivity.

At the heart of the emerging enlightenment concerning learning styles lies a mounting body of new information about the roles and functions of the right and left hemispheres of the human brain. For the first time, educators are beginning to understand the distinction between the characteristics and traits represented by the two hemispheres:

Left hemisphere functions	*Right hemisphere functions*
• Cognition	• Intuition
• Rationality	• Holistic style
• Logic	• Subjectivity
• Analytical style	• Imagination
• Factual orientation	• Spontaneity
• Sequential consciousness	• Simultaneous orientation
• Objectivity	• Fantasy

This knowledge provides a fresh approach to many problems of teacher ineffectiveness and student learning difficulties. It is now possible for many administrators, teachers, and parents to grasp why teaching and learning don't always correlate and how to establish greater efficiency in the teaching–learning act.

Although no one is totally dominated by either the left or the right hemisphere of the brain, all seem to have an intrinsic preferential reliance on one or the other, which obviously has considerable meaning for how individuals learn. In light of this fact, many individual teachers and entire school staffs are starting to alter their programs and approaches to provide a balanced educational environment easily accessible to learners of all types.

Differences in Learning Styles

In addition to the rich body of basic research on right and left brainedness, an increasing cumulation of studies continues to disclose a growing number of definitive differences in the patterns and styles by which teachers teach and pupils learn. Some of the most prevalent and clearly defined variances in individual styles include:

- Differences in perceptual modality preference (conceptual versus perceptual learning)
- Differences in attention styles (variances in the way individuals apply attention)
- Auditory versus visual learning styles
- Analytical versus global learning styles
- Differences in time rhythms (morning versus afternoon learners)
- Constricted versus flexible learning styles
- "Masculine" versus "feminine" behavioral styles
- Variances in memory processing

Of even more interest and practical value to some school staffs in unlocking doors to learning difficulties has been the work of Anthony Gregore (University of Connecticut), whose research has identified four distinctly different categories of preferred learning styles: (1) concrete–sequential learners, (2) concrete–random learners, (3) abstract–sequential learners, and (4) abstract–random learners.

Based on the information, knowledge, and understanding contained in the explosion of scientific study described above, administrators now have some new tools for helping teachers to improve their individual performance and for enhancing the effectiveness of the total school program.

Although many lessons remain to be learned from the study of brain function and personal learning styles, it is already clear that understanding how children learn is basic to educational improvement. School officials can do much to increase teacher and learner success by basing school betterment plans on these established facts:

- It is imperative that school personnel avoid confusing differences in style with differences in ability.
- Teachers teach best when using their own natural learning styles.
- Mismatches of teaching and learning styles affect teachers as well as students.

- Occasional exposure to differing styles can stretch students.
- An overmatching of teacher–learning styles can generate boredom and restlessness in students (and, occasionally, in teachers).
- Chronic mismatches of style can lead to emotional, behavioral, or mental problems on the part of students.
- Effective teachers must employ a mix of teaching techniques and strategies aimed at the entire range of individual learning styles.
- The principal's role in applying new concepts of individual learning styles is to remain up to date on current research findings, to provide appropriate staff development programs as needed, and to work toward a flexible learning environment in every classroom.

FIFTY WAYS TO MAKE EVERY TEACHER BETTER

One of the fundamental facets of a modern program of positive personnel management in schools must be a commitment to fostering and facilitating the best possible performance by every employee. This implies a willingness to make every effort to salvage weak personnel as well as to increase the productivity of everyone on the staff. Below are 50 clearcut actions any administrator can take to improve the effectiveness of teachers regardless of their current level of performance.

1. Use team teaching as a catalyst for change and improvement.
2. Promote visitations or observations in other schools.
3. Develop a job target approach to professional performance appraisal.
4. Minimize interruptions and pull-outs.
5. Consider "problem children" in making class assignments and determining individual class sizes (particularly at the elementary level). Provide management aides for classes with a high incidence of hyperactive pupils.
6. Conduct an aggressive building-level program of staff development and in-service based on individual needs.
7. Take specific steps to help teachers improve discipline in the classroom.
8. Select materials that stress individualization (pretests, posttests, enrichment activities, and so on).
9. Pilot a mini-release program for teachers to work with small groups. (Aides and intern teachers can be used for this purpose.)
10. Provide teachers with help in individualizing instruction.
11. Provide adequate manipulative materials for classroom use at all levels.
12. Encourage cross-grade-level teacher exchange programs.
13. Develop a clearcut job description for all teachers.
14. Help teachers to apply new research findings on teaching–learning styles.

15. Minimize paperwork and clerical chores for teachers (tame the paper tiger).

16. Encourage teachers to use learning contracts to help students know exactly what is expected.

17. Compile and distribute a collection of "promising practices" in the school or throughout the district.

18. Provide full-time social workers in each building to work with problem families and difficult school–home relationships.

19. Provide staff with continuous information on emerging future trends.

20. Provide teachers with up-to-date, easy-to-follow scope and sequence guides in all major subject areas.

21. Make room in your staffing pattern for one or more instructional program specialists (master teachers) to assist all teachers through curricular expertise, peer counseling, demonstration teaching, and so on (see sample job description in Figure 5–6).

22. Encourage teachers to use consumer (student, parent) evaluations wherever appropriate.

23. Foster use of community resources by providing every teacher with a directory of available volunteers.

24. Initiate grade-level meetings to discuss matters of mutual concern.

25. Introduce a time-on-task program emphasizing the importance of quality time—time spent on the right task (see list of factors affecting time on task in Figure 5–7).

26. Have a speaker phone available to every classroom.

27. Create a professional information center to communicate trends, exchange ideas, provide bibliographies, and so on.

28. Publicly recognize excellence in all areas of teaching.

29. Provide adequate microcomputers accessible to all grade levels.

30. Establish a "Floating Workshop Day" for schools at different levels (elementary, middle, junior high, senior high) to dismiss on different days to permit vertical visitations and observations.

31. Promote the use of personal conferences with pupils by teachers.

32. Make provisions for teachers to videotape their performance in the classroom and to view and critique privately.

33. Provide opportunities for teachers to become technologically literate (comfortable with computers, cablevision, and so on).

34. Instigate a process for staff members to nominate other teachers to share ideas and explain successful strategies at a weekly or monthly voluntary faculty meeting.

35. Train teachers in the skills of active listening.

Position: Elementary Instructional Program Specialist (K–6)

Responsible to: Assistant Superintendent

Responsibilities:

   1. Provide leadership and coordination in the development, implementation, and evaluation of the K–6 instructional program.
   2. Serve as an additional liaison between the elementary staff and district administration.
   3. Consult with elementary staff regarding program planning, classroom organization, teaching techniques, and available resources.
   4. Initiate and promote the exchange of sound instructional programs and techniques, including demonstration teaching as appropriate.
   5. Assist in developing and providing appropriate staff development programs for the elementary staff.
   6. Promote a climate of positive school–community relations and provide information to the community about the elementary instructional program.
   7. Provide leadership in carrying out mandated and optional transition team recommendations for the implementation of the pairing concept of elementary organization.
   8. Provide consultation for the development of individual teacher job targets, ICP projects, building grant proposals, and building-level minicourses.
   9. Provide supervision and direction for the elementary instructional aide.
  10. Perform such other duties as assigned by the assistant superintendent.

Figure 5–6

FACTORS AFFECTING TIME ON TASK

- Absences and tardiness
- Interruptions
- Pull-out programs
- Discipline problems
- Organization and management of the classroom.
- Teaching strategies

Figure 5–7

36. Demonstrate how teachers can use games constructively in the classroom (anything that entails an answer can be transformed into a game).

37. Direct a greater portion of the building or district budget from expenditures for texts and workbooks to the purchase of process-oriented equipment (manipulatives, artifacts, and so on).

38. Start a building-level wellness program (install an exercise bike, establish a wellness assessment center, begin building a fitness library, and so on).

39. Help teachers to mix their teaching strategies by introducing a plan for logging and recording activities within the classroom.

40. Provide in-service training on time management for teachers.

41. Help teachers to arrange intergenerational experiences for students.

42. Consider an annual competition for the best teaching ideas and innovations. Offer prizes.

43. Encourage shirt-sleeve learning, an emphasis on action or service learning rather than passive pupil involvement.

44. Provide teachers with a model daily schedule that includes some self-directed time for all pupils.

45. Initiate a program of voluntary peer review.

46. Establish a teacher idea center within the school or district offering a wide range of supplemental and enrichment materials, games, and project ideas available for checkout.

47. Introduce a program of curriculum tracking to assist teachers in understanding the hidden curriculum operating within the school.

48. Arrange for PTSA-sponsored mini-grants to encourage action–research projects within the classroom.

49. Develop daily schedules that accommodate grade-level or team planning.

50. Introduce a voluntary program of lesson-plan review and comment by peers on an anonymous basis.

All of the suggestions above can contribute to a successful program for improving the proficiency and productivity of strong and weak teachers alike.

ACTION STEPS IN IMPROVING TEACHER–PARENT RELATIONS

In working to improve marginal teachers, school officials should recognize that in certain circumstances an image of ineffectiveness may be perceived rather than real. Sometimes a teacher may be marked by an unearned reputation for being substandard because of poor rapport and relationships with parents and not because of any real lack of success with students.

When this is the case, the task of the administrator or supervisor is to assist the teacher in promoting positive home–school relations, making parents aware of the teacher's true strengths, and involving the community constructively in the classroom program.

Examples of Successful Communication Models

Examples of successful techniques for establishing a positive image program are contained in the following school-tested communication models, which can strengthen the perceived effectiveness of any teacher:

- Grade-level parent meetings
- Home visitations by teachers
- "Sunshine" telephone calls to convey accolades and anecdotes
- An open door policy with specific days (or every day if feasible) set aside as visiting days for parents
- Periodic classroom newsletters and calendars of special events and activities (including tips on how parents can support and participate)
- An exceptional trait record to offer parents an opportunity to state traits and characteristics they believe make their children unique
- A word-a-day program involving parents and students in defining, using, and illustrating new vocabulary words on a daily basis
- Encouraging parents to be reading partners with their children
- A prior experience assessment to help teachers discover student interests and abilities and to plan accordingly
- A learning fair to demonstrate classroom materials and techniques as well as resources available for parents to assist with student learning

CHAPTER SUPPLEMENTS

The following chapter supplements are included to illustrate the principles outlined in this chapter.

Contents:

- A Dozen Discipline Principles for Principals
- Sample "Learning Fair" Flyer

A DOZEN DISCIPLINE PRINCIPLES FOR PRINCIPALS*

1. The basis for discipline is effective instruction. Positive behavior is a by-product of sound teaching.

2. Schools are not intrinsically all good or all bad. Every school and every classroom is a mix of positive and negative factors.

3. Individualized discipline is as important as individualized instruction. Fair and equal discipline does not demand that everyone receive exactly the same treatment or punishment.

4. The only way to change behavior is through feelings.

5. Nothing improves unless there is involvement on the part of staff, students, and parents.

6. Most students want to achieve, to get along with others, and to go along with reasonable rules.

7. The inappropriate actions of children and youth are largely products of how adults treat them (at home and at school).

8. Victimization is reduced in schools characterized by close teacher–principal cooperation.

9. The principal must know the law. Innocent omissions or inadvertent violations of due process can jeopardize any single disciplinary decision or action, the overall effectiveness of the school's total discipline program, and, more importantly, the administrator's entire future career.

10. One teacher whose class or classroom is completely out of control can affect the entire school. The principal must exercise every means possible to maintain a subtle revolving door for incompetents and to weed out any discipline duds on the staff.

11. The principal does not have to be the best teacher in the building, but the principal must know what good teaching is and must have the skills necessary to help all teachers get better.

12. When caught in a crossfire of conflicting views, the principal's first choice of action should always be determined by what's best for the student, now and in the future.

---

*Robert D. Ramsey, *Educator's Discipline Handbook* West Nyack, N.Y.: (Parker Publishing Company, Inc., 1981), p. 44.

SAMPLE "LEARNING FAIR" FLYER

LEARNING: IT'S A FAMILY A-FAIR!

1983 Learning Fair

Learning Learning Learning Learning Learning Lea

ST. LOUIS PARK SCHOOLS

TUESDAY

MARCH 15, 1983

2:00 P.M.-8:30 P.M.

CENTRAL SCHOOL

CAFETERIA

6300 WALKER

Come to the Learning Fair!

Displays, demonstrations, handouts, hands-on opportunities on the computer and more, all focusing on things you can do at home to help your child.

Staff members will be on hand to answer questions and give mini-presentations in a variety of academic skill areas. A variety of handouts with suggestions about how to help your children in the curriculum areas also will be available.

To prepare an adequate number of brochures, hand-outs, and plan for refreshments please return the bottom portion of this sheet.

- -

Please return to your elementary school by Wednesday, February 16, 1983.

_____ Number planning to attend
_____ Unsure at this time
_____ Unable to attend
Our children are in the following grades:

_____ preschool	_____ grade three
_____ kindergarten	_____ grade four
_____ grade one	_____ grade five
_____ grade two	_____ grade six

Signed _____ School _____

6

Practical Ways
to Revitalize
Veteran Teachers

Changing times and maturing staffs have imposed a new dimension on personnel management in the public schools. In addition to the traditional personnel roles required of school leaders (negotiations, contract administration, grievance processing, and so on), staff renewal and the continuous development of the school's human resources have become critical survival functions for effective educational managers in the 1980s.

Although renewal is ultimately a personal quest, organizational leaders can assist in the process by providing stimulus, opportunities for growth, and a facilitative environment. Obviously, there is no simple recipe for renewal or revitalization. Nevertheless, most successful programs of staff development encompass the following features:

- Concrete and specific objectives
- An emphasis on application and practicality
- Principal involvement
- Opportunities for individualization
- Easy access (held on school sites)
- A commitment to ongoing development

In most instances, the initial step in formulating a comprehensive program of staff renewal must be to conduct some form of assessment of employee interests and needs. A sample inventory instrument designed to identify potential topics for staff development in the area of personal wellness appears in Figure 6–1.

STAGES OF PROFESSIONAL LIFE

In education, as in other professions, most individuals follow a common pattern of personal and professional development. Effective administrators tailor their staff development efforts to match the maturity level of the individuals involved and the total staff in general. The most prevalent phases of individual and staff maturation are depicted in the profile in Figure 6–2.

THE TWOFOLD TARGET: STAFF DEVELOPMENT AND SELF-DEVELOPMENT

Traditional programs of staff development have focused almost exclusively on subject area content, teaching techniques, and instructional skills. Increasingly, however, educational leaders are becoming aware that ongoing renewal can be achieved only if the staff members involved are encouraged and enabled to develop as fully functioning persons, as well as technically equipped professionals. The twofold target of an effective staff revitalization program for the 1980s is (1) staff development (traditional instructional improvement activities) and (2) self-development (self-analysis and personal growth). A modern program for comprehensive staff renewal analyzes needs for both personal and professional development and attempts to respond to all of these needs.

A PRACTICAL DESIGN FOR PROMOTING STAFF WELLNESS

One of the most recent areas of emphasis in school staff development programs is attention to employee wellness. As in many businesses and industries, a growing number of school districts are recognizing the importance of investing in the improvement of employee physical and mental health.

An ambitious wellness development program for all employees can serve as the centerpiece of the school's overall staff development activity. Such efforts reflect management's concern for individual employees and can result in enormous payoffs in morale and productivity. The objective of a health promotion program is to maximize employee well-being and sense of personal worth and power. Most effective employee wellness programs are based on three fundamental concepts:

1. Wellness is unique within each person.
2. Wellness is first and foremost an attitude.
3. Total wellness encompasses many dimensions (holistic health, lifestyle management, risk education, self-help, self-care, nutrition, physical fitness, environmental concerns, stress management, and so on).

INTEREST INVENTORY FOR
STAFF DEVELOPMENT
AND SELF-DEVELOPMENT

Please indicate your level of interest in each of the following topics for potential staff development programs.

	No Interest	Information Only	Group Activities	Confidential (Personal) Assistance
Physical				
Fitness	___	___	___	___
Stop-smoking programs	___	___	___	___
Exercise programs	___	___	___	___
Weight reduction	___	___	___	___
Nutrition	___	___	___	___
Healthy sexual function	___	___	___	___
Spiritual/philosophical				
Value clarification	___	___	___	___
Lifestyle assessment	___	___	___	___
Motivation	___	___	___	___
Environmental				
Safety	___	___	___	___
Environmental impact on wellness	___	___	___	___
Estate planning	___	___	___	___
Relationships				
Communication skills	___	___	___	___
Relationship building	___	___	___	___
Parenting skills	___	___	___	___
Marriage enrichment	___	___	___	___
Coping with a two-career couple	___	___	___	___
Single parenting function	___	___	___	___

Figure 6–1

Job-Related

Time management	____	____	____	____
Job change	____	____	____	____
Organizational team building	____	____	____	____
Improving organizational health	____	____	____	____
Retirement planning	____	____	____	____
Résumé preparation	____	____	____	____
Interviewing skills	____	____	____	____
Dealing with sexism	____	____	____	____

Psychological

Relaxation	____	____	____	____
Stress management	____	____	____	____
Depression	____	____	____	____
Drug abuse	____	____	____	____
Conflict management	____	____	____	____
Assertiveness training	____	____	____	____
Crisis management	____	____	____	____
Death and dying	____	____	____	____
Self-discipline	____	____	____	____
Meditation	____	____	____	____

Figure 6–1 *(continued)*

LEVELS OF PROFESSIONAL LIFE

Level I.   Establishment, provisional professionalism ("Young Turks")
Level II.   Mature pro (Being your own person)
Level III. "Middlesence" (Mid-career transition or crisis)
Level IV.   Mentoring (Contentment or disillusionment)*

---

*Sometimes, morale and productivity are greatest among mature professionals who have made peace with themselves and with the limits of their profession.

Figure 6–2

Listed below is a sampling of suggestions for conducting a well-rounded wellness program, which have been collected from successful practices in several leading school systems across the country:

- Make school facilities (pools, gymnasiums, courts, tracks, bike racks, weight rooms) available for individual staff fitness activities.
- Open schools for early morning jogging.
- Encourage staff members to maintain their own health records in a highly mobile society.
- Permit teachers to use prep time for physical activity.
- Offer hypertension (blood pressure) screening in each school.
- Involve all employees (licensed and classified personnel) in the health promotion program.
- Establish a staff wellness committee and allocate funds for the committee's activities.
- Sponsor weight reduction programs for interested staff members.
- Provide exercise bikes in each school for employee use during the work day.
- Conduct stop-smoking programs.
- Offer self-protection training.
- Encourage the use of lifestyle assessment forms by all employees.
- Promote CPR (cardiopulmonary resuscitation) training for staff members at all levels.
- Establish a circulating wellness library.
- Promote fruit-juice breaks.
- Provide in-service courses on nutrition education, safety training, biofeedback, anger management, using biorhythms to anticipate ups and downs, time management, relaxation techniques, family survival, and so on.
- Provide a quiet time room for staff use.
- Offer courses in aerobic exercise.
- Sponsor staff softball, bowling, or volleyball teams.
- Develop videotape demonstrations of fitness activities for use by individual staff members and faculty groups.
- Make drug abuse counseling available to all employees at no cost and with complete confidentiality.
- Hold periodic golf tournaments open to all employees.
- Encourage faculty "fun runs" and walkathons.
- Offer cost-free cancer checks in each building at periodic intervals.

- Establish staff support and discussion groups.
- Promote a "get-out-at-noon" program.
- Encourage the use of a personal wellness contract to identify individual fitness action plans.
- Offer T-shirts to participants in all school-sponsored wellness activities.
- Establish a regular staff newsletter devoted to wellness information (see example in Figure 6–3).

TWENTY-FIVE REMEDIES FOR STAFF STRESS

In education, as in most service professions, one of the major emerging wellness challenges is the management of employee stress and the avoidance of teacher burnout. During a pivotal period of change, demands and expectations are continually increasing for an ever-maturing teacher corps across the country. This has led many observers to view the potential stress mess among professional educators as a critical concern to those responsible for effective personnel management.

Obviously, some level of stress is essential and universal. In many instances, stress is a positive life factor and serves as a valuable "smoke detector" within the individual. Nevertheless, in western cultures, particularly the United States, stress and burnout seem to be taking an increasing toll on employee performance and effectiveness. This is especially true in jobs, such as teaching and school administration, where people are responsible for other people.

In most school settings, there is an array of potential stressors inherent in the responsibilities of teachers and administrators which can impair personal and professional performances. A partial list of these contributors to unhealthy stress is as follows:

- Isolation
- Discipline problems
- Community pressures
- Lack of time
- Administrative demands
- Paperwork
- Mandates
- Red tape
- Regulations
- Lack of "strokes"
- Junk mail
- Media treatment
- Financial worries
- Child drain
- Parental demands
- Class size
- Deadlines
- Negotiations
- Legal problems
- Overload
- Militant peer pressure
- Grievances
- Evaluations
- Phone calls
- "Reportomania"
- Home problems

You Don't Have To Be Sick To Get Better!

A Publication Dedicated to the Physical & Mental Health of St. Louis Park School's Employees.

WHAT A YEAR FOR SD^2!

Whew! What a first year for the Staff Development/Self Development Committee. The Committee worked hard all year to bring the kinds of activities you really wanted to our schools.

Do you remember all of these activities?

Opening Day Convocation - Brian Willette
Needs Assessment Conducted
Retirement Seminar on TRA
Aerobics with Amy Lee
Wellness Seminar with Dick Shafer
Time Management Seminar
FUNDAY
Stress Workshops with Methodist Hospital
P.E.R.A. Seminar
Career Alternatives Workshop
Assault/Burglary Workshops
Career Center Open House
Discipline Without Tears Workshop
Career Change Workshop
Monthly newsletter
SD^2 Bulletin Boards
Food Service Recognition Day
50 Mile Club
Exercise Bikes in each school
Fitness tests offered to staff

We are already looking forward to next year. This is what is already scheduled for next year:

Opening Workshop Day--will be held at the Jr. High with a breakfast before the speaker. The speaker will be James E. Weigand, Dean of School of Continuing Studies at Indiana University. He is a human behavior researcher. He'll talk to us about respect for others, self confidence, sensitivity to the needs of others, service and optimism.

Following the speaker, each employee will be able to take a lifestyle assessment in cooperation with the St. Louis Park Medical Center.

A workshop is scheduled in September on the topic "Building Positive Relationships."

The SD^2 Committee welcomes your suggestions for activities for next year.

Have a healthy summer! See you next August!

I'D PICK MORE DAISIES

If I had my life to live over, I'd try to make more mistakes next time. I would limber up. I would be sillier than I have been this trip. I know of very few things I would take seriously. I would be crazier. I would be less hygenic. I would climb more mountains, swim more rivers and watch more sunsets. I would eat more ice cream and less beans. I would have more active troubles and fewer imaginary ones. You see, I am one of those people who lives life sensibly and sanely, hour after hour, day after day. Oh, I have had my moments, and if I had it to do over again, I'd have more of them. In fact, I'd try to have nothing else. Just moments, one after another, instead of living so many years ahead each day. I have been one of those people who never go anywhere without a thermometer, a hot-water bottle, a gargle, a raincoat and a parachute. If I had it to do over again, I would go places and do things and travel lighter. If I had my life to live over, I would start bare-footed earlier in the spring and stay that way later in the fall. I would play hooky more. I wouldn't make such good grades except by accident. I would ride on more merry-go-rounds. I'd pick more daisies.

Author Unknown

Figure 6-3

YOU ARE WHAT YOU EAT

You are probably tired of hearing about
it. Americans today are the most diet-
conscious people in the world. Yet over
half of us are still overweight. Most
of us every day consume foods which many
nutritionists now believe actually cause
long-term damage to our health.

The secrets of healthy eating -- and
dieting -- are balance and variety.
This is a far more efficient way of
reaching and maintaining the right
weight than going on crash or "fad" diets.
Crash or "fad" diets usually result in
rapid weight loss but then the weight
is usually regained just as fast. There's
medical evidence showing that this yo-yo
effect puts a strain on your health.

No matter how nutritious your diet is,
you'll gain weight if your appetite is
too large for the amount of energy you
consume. There is only one way to lose
weight: Eat less and burn more energy.
But shedding weight doesn't have to be
agony.

Regardless of your previous experience
with dieting, if you eat only 300 fewer
calories than you did the day before,
you will lose one pound every 12 days.

Suggestions to conscientious dieters who
really mean business:

If the place where you usually lunch
offers a menu that is a constant tempta-
tion, bring a lunch from home or start
exploring less congenial restaurants.

If your regular lunch companions or
members of your family are big meal
eaters, try to eat alone as much as
possible.

It's true that these
measures can deprive
you of congenial com-
pany and also of
personal contacts you
may enjoy. Balance
that risk against the
demonstrable risk to
your health of being
overweight, and you
have an incentive to
find a way to stick to
your diet, regardless
of where you are and
whom you are with.

HOW TO BEHAVE IF TAKEN HOSTAGE

While the idea of being taken hostage may
seem farfetched, it's happening with dis-
concerting frequency in many big cities,
especially in banks, liquor stores and
airplanes. Frank Bolz, captain of the
New York City Police Hostage Negotiating
Team gives these tips to get through it
safely:

* Concentrate on following instructions
  exactly during the first 15-45 minutes.
  This is the critical period when the
  terrorist is emotional and trigger-happy.

* Keep quiet and speak only when spoken to.
  Don't try to be friendly, phony, argumen-
  tative or hostile.

* Don't make suggestions. Reason: captors
  will suspect a trick.

* Be wary of attempting escape. If it
  fails, it's likely to bring violence.

* If you are released ahead of others,
  closely observe everything that goes on
  in order to help police.

* Treat the hostage-takers like royalty,
  but try not to be over condescending.

* Expect to be frisked or even treated
  roughly by police when released. Cooper-
  ate fully. Reason: police aren't sure
  who is who and they don't take chances.

WHEN BOTH SPOUSES WORK

A fair division of household tasks is
crucial. One approach: select the
mutually most-hated tasks and hire some-
one to do as many of them as possible.
Negotiate the remaining disliked jobs.

Don't alternate jobs. That
only leads to arguments
about whose turn it is.
Schedule quarterly or semi-
annual reviews for adjustments and trade-offs.

Have a good summer!

Figure 6-3 (continued)

Long-term exposure to the relentless presence of such pressures can produce serious stress problems and burnout (combat fatigue) among the professional staff. In schools, as in most work environments, some of the most common manifestations and symptoms of negative stress are neglected responsibilities, depression on the job, perfunctory performance, increased absenteeism, and tension among employees at all levels.

Ultimately, each individual must address and resolve his or her own personal problems of stress. Nevertheless, there are a host of measures school officials can take to help staff members handle stress, to provide support during periods of pronounced stress, and to establish a climate that minimizes the destructive impact of unhealthy stress on employees.

The following is a list of 25 stress management strategies that have been helpful to individuals and groups in many schools and other professional groups:

1. Associate with positive people—avoid chronic complainers.
2. Pay attention to proper diet and nutritional needs.
3. Prioritize and simplify your personal and professional life.
4. Engage in a regular exercise program.
5. Insist on sufficient rest and sleep.
6. Learn to delegate.
7. Talk about problems—don't bottle up feelings.
8. Leave teaching at school.
9. Get regular physical checkups.
10. Learn time management skills—don't become overcalendared.
11. Interact with people who make you feel good.
12. Give your emotions some down time each day.
13. Develop hobbies and other outside interests.
14. Find a private retreat at school (even a restroom may do).
15. Break the inertia barrier—begin to do something about problems in your life.
16. Develop friendships outside education.
17. Use summer job opportunities to associate with adults.
18. Loaf a little.
19. Learn to say no.
20. Use guided imagery (picture something relaxing) to ease tension.
21. Reward yourself for achievement and completion of difficult tasks.
22. Engage in relaxation exercises during the school day.
23. Develop support networks with other professionals.
24. Design your own personal wellness contract including specific steps to improve your life style or physical well-being.
25. Take a leave when necessary.

SAMPLES OF SUCCESSFUL IN-SERVICE PROGRAMS

All of the wellness measures described here can make a major contribution to staff revitalization. As stated earlier, however, an up-to-date program of staff renewal requires balance and attention to both staff development and self-development. This final portion of the chapter provides examples of a wealth of workshop ideas and in-service programs that have been successful in meeting this twofold goal.

In designing an effective overall program of staff development and self-development, a number of school leaders have found the following five guidelines to be helpful:

1. The total staff (administrators, teachers, classified personnel) and parents should be included wherever appropriate.
2. All levels of the staff should participate in identifying needs and developing programs.
3. The overall program should provide for a variety of growth experiences (varied times, locales, presentation styles, and so on).
4. The program should be personalized or at least targeted toward individual building staffs wherever possible.
5. Throughout the program, both individual and group needs should be addressed.

The components of a successful in-service program should be selected with care to provide balance and to satisfy these criteria.

Figure 6–4 is a sample of successful workshop and in-service topics and programs offered in one school system over a two-year period. Individually, each of these efforts provided some worthwhile growth opportunities. More importantly, however, collectively these components reflected a cohesive and comprehensive overall program aimed at meeting both the personal and professional in-service needs (staff development and self-development) of the entire staff.

One further example of a holistic approach to in-service training is reflected in Figure 6–5, the announcement of an exemplary staff development project.

In addition to a balanced offering of pertinent workshops and other training sessions, one of the earmarks of a workable program for revitalization is an action-oriented approach that enables veteran teachers to try their wings in new ventures without fear of failure. Where mature staffs have outgrown interest and enthusiasm for traditional in-service courses and after-school workshops, significant renewal sometimes can be stimulated by allocating a portion of the district's staff development budget for mini-grants awarded to individuals or groups of teachers who engage in piloting innovative classroom practices. A model for such a mini-grant program is outlined in Figure 6–6.

Another workable approach to renewal for maturing staffs is to allocate a fraction of district in-service funds for use by individual building or department

A SAMPLER OF SUCCESSFUL
WORKSHOP AND IN-SERVICE
TOPICS AND PROGRAMS

- Teaching Styles—Learning Styles
- Cooperative Learning
- Focus on Time Management
- Effective Discipline: Building Positive Relationships
- Individualizing Education
- Managing Everyday Life
- Eating Well and Enjoying It
- Life-style Assessment
- Career Alternatives Workshop
- Stress Management Workshop
- Learning Styles in the Classroom
- Feeling Fit, Feeling Fine
- Protecting Yourself from Personal Assault
- Estate Planning for Professionals
- Discipline without Tears
- Never Resign on Monday: How to Cope with Stress in the 1980s
- Deciding to Be Yourself
- Getting Along with Yourself and Others
- Keeping Your Head Above Water
- File, Don't Pile
- Implications of Teaching Styles and Learning Styles for Curriculum

Figure 6–4

'Developing the 21st Century Educator'

GOAL:

To plan and implement a staff development program designed to equip staff members to meet the needs of students in the 21st Century as envisioned by Project '85 of the St. Louis Park Public Schools.

ACTIVITIES AND OBJECTIVES:

- to enable educators to identify their teaching styles out of the four identified by Dr. Anthony Gregorc;
- to begin to identify their students' learning styles (appropriate instruments are still in developmental stage);
- to provide educators, through inservice, with assistance in varying their teaching styles in order to match and stretch their students' learning styles;
- to provide educators with knowledge about recent brain research and an awareness of the need to teach right brain activities;
- to identify instructional situations which can be delivered more efficiently and effectively via technology such as microcomputers and closed circuit telecast capability.

PROCESSES:

- offer inservice workshops with acknowledged experts in the areas of learning and teaching styles, brain research and instructional techniques.
- provide release time to enable teachers to attend workshops and revise curriculum.

OUTCOMES:

- teachers will vary their current teaching styles and adapt curriculum materials in order to reach to all four learning styles identified by Gregorc.
- teachers will explore and expand their use of instructional techniques.
- a manual to assist other districts with planning and implementing similar staff development programs will be developed.

Figure 6–5

INNOVATIVE CLASSROOM PRACTICES PROGRAM

The Innovative Classroom Practices Program (ICP) is intended to provide seed money for the promotion and encouragement of unique or innovative practices developed by classroom teachers within our school district. The program provides individual grants of up to $500 for one year on a nonrenewable basis. Proposals for funding are reviewed by a committee consisting of teachers and administrators and are judged on the basis of the criteria outlined below.

Criteria for Approval

The following criteria serve as the basis for consideration of ICP proposals:

1. The project must be classroom-based with direct impact on students.
2. The project must indicate good potential for replication in other classroom settings if successful.
3. The project may involve more than one classroom or more than one staff member.
4. The $500 is the maximum amount of a single ICP award. It is possible to consider a joint award if the projects involved clearly entail the interaction of more than one teacher and more than one class.
5. The awards are nonrenewable and are available for one year only; therefore, they should not involve recurring costs.
6. The awards will be based on a demonstrable need for funding at the level requested.
7. The projects should be innovative in their approach, strategy, or delivery system.
8. The funds can be used to provide for materials, services, and so on; they cannot be used to provide for payments for the proposing teacher or for travel purposes. (While the funding available cannot be used to employ personnel per se, the funds can be used for personal services such as an artist in residence, limited consulting service, and so on).
9. Individuals assigned to other than classrooms (social workers, counselors, and others) may apply, but their application must be in conjunction with and countersigned by a classroom teacher.

Proposal Format

The proposals should be simple and straightforward in nature, limited to no more than two or three pages, and should cover the following areas:

Figure 6–6

Identification of need

Objectives and outcomes
of the project

Individuals or groups involved

Time period

Estimated budget

Evaluation procedures

Examples of Programs

The funds for ICP are not intended to serve interests outside the classroom or those that do not directly affect students. The type of program this funding is intended to support would include interdisciplinary program efforts, programs for the gifted and talented, unique or innovative delivery systems, basic skills, affective education, chemical dependency programs, and individualization of instruction. The foregoing constitutes a partial but certainly not exclusive list of the types of programs likely to be approved for ICP funding.

Figure 6–6 *(continued)*

staffs under a program of staff development mini-grants. This approach often has particular appeal to veteran teacher groups in that it features involvement, individualization, and responsiveness to practical felt needs at the building level. Examples of a model building-level staff development mini-grant program and a sample application form appear in Figure 6–7 and 6–8.

All of these ideas and examples point up ways to shape a well-balanced program of staff development and renewal which can be applied in any district regardless of size or level of staff maturity.

STAFF DEVELOPMENT MINI-GRANT PROGRAM

Preface

The mini-grant program is meant to facilitate and enhance an ongoing process, not to be a one-time enlightening experience that is then filed and forgotten. As you consider options, please think about the crucial concern that has been expressed by many faculty members and staff development experts about implementation and follow-up. You should be considering a process that could continue in subsequent years.

Background Information

As you think about preparing mini-grant applications, the following information may be helpful to you.

> More than one building, program, or department can jointly develop a grant proposal.
>
> There are many ways to structure staff development activities. Examples include use of release time through substitutes, use of a consultant (who could be anyone from a national expert to one of our own internal experts), or use of after-school, evening, or Saturday time.

Funding

As funds are limited, priority will be given to building-level requests according to the following guidelines:

Elementary centers	$ 800
Junior High	$1000
Senior High	$1300

Figure 6–7

BUILDING OR PROGRAM LEVEL
MINI-GRANT APPLICATION

School/program_____Amount requested_____

1. What are the priorities or goals to which your grant proposal is being addressed?
2. Briefly describe the process by which this grant application was developed.
3. Describe the program and activities for which you are requesting funding.
4. How many staff members do you anticipate would participate in the above?
5. What are your plans for implementation and follow-up?
6. Describe what you would consider to be evidence of successful implementation.
7. Detail the budget for your proposal.

Date_____ Signed_____

_____
(Building principal, if applicable)

_____
(Department chair, if applicable)

Please return to Personnel Office.

Figure 6—8

CHAPTER SUPPLEMENTS

The following chapter supplements are included to illustrate the principles outlined in this chapter.

Contents:

- A "Wellness" Bibliography for School Personnel
- Sample Professional Leave Guidelines

A "WELLNESS" BIBLIOGRAPHY FOR SCHOOL PERSONNEL

Ardell, D. B. High-Level Wellness. Emmaus, Penn.: Rodale Press, 1981.

Burns, David D. Feeling Good. New York: New American Library, 1980.

Cousins, Norman. Anatomy of an Illness. New York: Norton and Company, 1981.

Davis, Adelle. Let's Stay Healthy. New York: Harcourt, Brace, Jovanovich, Inc., 1981.

Hastings, Arthur, et al. Health for the Whole Person. Boulder, Colo.: Westview Press, 1980.

Kübler-Ross, Elizabeth. Holistic Ways to Health and Happiness. New York: Simon and Schuster, 1981.

Lakein, Alan. How to Get Control of Your Time and Your Life. New York: New American Library, 1981.

Miller, G. P. Life Choices. New York: Bantam, 1981.

Potter, Beverly A. Beating Job Burnout. San Francisco: Harbor Publishing Company, 1980.

Powell, John. Fully Human—Fully Alive. Allen Tex.: Argus, 1981.

SAMPLE PROFESSIONAL LEAVE GUIDELINES

In times of diminishing resources, it is imperative to strive for maximum return from staff development funds devoted to professional growth through participation in local, state, regional, and national conferences and conventions. The following sample guidelines illustrate procedures for distributing limited travel funds in an equitable manner and with optional benefit to the district and the individuals involved.

Professional leave may be granted to staff members in order to attend educational conferences and professional meetings, visit other schools, or execute special assignments for the benefit of the school system. Such approved absence shall be without loss of pay and shall not be deducted from basic or accumulated leave. Further, a substitute shall be provided when necessary, and expenses incurred shall be reimbursed in accord with the established guidelines and rules.

> Visitations within the school district or to other school districts, not to exceed one day and where no expenses are involved other than mileage, may be approved by the building principal, with reasonable limitations. These requests are not the responsibility of the Professional Leave Committee.

> Professional leave involving individuals who have been given a special assignment may be granted by the director of human resources and staff development.

> In all other cases, professional leave shall be granted by the director of human resources and staff development after approval by the Professional Leave Committee.

The Professional Leave Committee, composed of teachers and administrators, shall meet regularly to consider professional leave applications within their jurisdiction. All professional leave requests approved by the Professional Leave Committee require the endorsement of the director of human resources and staff development.

The guidelines and rules governing the granting of professional leave are as follows.

Determining Eligibility

1. Since wide participation in the professional leave program is desirable, it is expected that there will be no monopoly by any individual or department on the limited funds available.

2. The meeting or conference to be attended must be of value and must offer potential benefits directly to the applicant's assignment or the school system as a whole.

3. Where membership in the organization sponsoring the meeting is available, an applicant, to receive priority consideration for approval, should be a current member.

SAMPLE PROFESSIONAL LEAVE GUIDELINES (Continued)

4. Generally, those who are serving their first year in the district will not be eligible for professional leave. However, professional interest and ability to make a specific contribution are factors that may be considered in permitting an exception.

5. Generally, approval will be given to an applicant who is (1) an officer or committee chairman of the professional organization sponsoring the meeting, (2) invited to be an active participant in the program, or (3) requested by the administration to attend.

6. Except as the needs of a department or developing area or other special circumstances dictate, no more than two persons will be granted approval to attend the same meeting.

7. Time away from duty is to be considered. Except in extreme circumstances, no request will be approved that involves an absence of more than five work days. To minimize travel time, those attending meetings at a distance of more than 450 miles one way are expected to use public transportation if at all possible.

8. Whenever a staff member receives an expense allowance or fee for participating in a meeting, the professional leave application should be solely in the form of a request to be absent, except to the extent that the outside allowance or fee does not cover recognizable expenses.

9. Attendance at summer meetings or workshops will not be approved as professional leave unless the director of human resources and staff development determines that the expenses involved are to be reimbursed under the professional leave program.

10. Attendance of delegates of NEA, AFT, and their affiliates and similar meetings will be approved or disapproved directly by the superintendent. In such cases, no expenses will be allowed, although any substitutes required will be provided.

11. If approval of a leave request is denied because of depletion of funds, a staff member, with the expressed consent of the director of human resources and staff development, may assume the expenses of attending the meeting, including the cost of a substitute. Such approved absence shall be without loss of pay and shall not be deducted from basic or accumulated leave.

Application Process

1. Requests for all professional leave (national, regional, state, and local) shall be submitted on the "Application for Professional Leave," available in each building office.

2. Requests of teachers to attend national conventions shall be made in writing to the director of human resources and staff development for

SAMPLE PROFESSIONAL LEAVE GUIDELINES (Continued)

review by the Professional Leave Committee. Such requests shall be made as early in the school year as possible before October 1. Maximum reimbursement for travel and lodging expenses shall be set at $350.

Because funds available for professional leave are decreasing and the Professional Leave Committee endorses using those funds to assist as many staff members as possible, requests to attend local and regional conferences will receive higher priority than requests to attend national conferences held out of state. However, high priority will be given to attending a national convention held within the metro area.

3. Requests to attend state and local meetings shall be submitted as early as possible, and late applications are more likely to be denied. Substitutes and mileage will be provided for meetings in the greater seven-county area. Maximum reimbursement for travel and lodging at a state or regional convention shall be set at $75.

4. The principal must give prior approval to all applications forms for the elementary teacher. Both principal and department head must give prior approval to all application forms for secondary teachers. Specialists and instructional personnel not assigned to a building should be approved by their appropriate supervisors. Those specialists whose travel expenses are covered by the assistant superintendent's budget need not apply to the Professional Leave Committee.

5. An applicant whose leave application is approved will be so informed by the director of human resources and staff development. If a request is not approved, the Professional Leave Committee will inform the applicant, giving the reasons for the denial. In each case, a copy of the notification will be sent to the appropriate administrator or department head.

Reimbursement of Expenses

All expense statements must be submitted on the expense form and require the approval of the director of human resources and staff development. Specific expenses in the following categories shall be considered as approvable expenses. Expenses incurred other than for travel and lodging shall be the responsibility of the leave participant. Registration fees shall not be reimbursed. In order to receive reimbursement for approved expenses, the participant must submit all receipts for expenses at the same time.

Transportation

1. Car mileage shall be reimbursed according to the master agreement.
2. Air travel should be at the tourist or economy rate whenever feasible. Reservations should be arranged through the supervisor of fiscal operations in the business office.

SAMPLE PROFESSIONAL LEAVE GUIDELINES (Continued)

3. Whenever available, travel fare receipts are to be attached to the expense statement.

Lodging

1. Reasonable costs of lodging will be reimbursed. The lowest available rate should be requested. In order for the participant to qualify for reimbursement for lodging, the conference must not be within a reasonable commuting distance from his or her home.
2. Receipts for lodging must be attached to the expense statement.

Reporting

Upon returning, each person granted a professional leave privilege may be requested to submit a brief written report to the appropriate administrators, departments, or department heads. The director of human resources and staff development will ask each person to submit a written report on a form to be provided by the personnel office.

7

The Nuts and Bolts of Handling Teacher Strikes

The acid test of any personnel management program comes during and after the time of a strike by any employee group, but this is particularly true in the event of a teacher's strike.

Many of the personnel management practices described throughout this guide are designed to avert the kind of divisive working relations that create a strike situation. Nevertheless, local circumstances sometimes result in a strike climate despite the best preventive measures.

Obviously, the incidence of teacher strikes in this country has increased dramatically during the past decade and probably will continue to do so as long as positive benefits result for the striking participants. Expanded legislative provision for strikes by public employees, continued growth in power by national teacher organizations, and the advent of a new breed in the educational work force have all contributed to the proliferation of strikes in the nation's schools.

Where legislation permits, administrators must realize that the strike is the ultimate weapon in the arsenal of the teacher's union or organization, and it may be used. All strikes are difficult, some are devastating, but none are the end of the world. No matter how strained and emotional a strike scene may become, it's important that administrators remember that the strike will end sometime.

ELEMENTS OF A SUCCESSFUL STRIKE PLAN

One mark of a truly professional personnel management program is the development of a comprehensive strike plan, which ideally will never be employed, but when necessary can minimize the pain, avoid costly errors, and ease the return to normalcy when the strike is over. Planning is essential for the successful management of a strike situation and a rapid recovery following a work stoppage of any duration.

Obviously, effective plans are more readily developed during a period of relative calm rather than in an emotion-laden atmosphere once a strike is imminent or under way.

It behooves all administrators at the district and building level to think ahead in compiling as comprehensive a set of plans and procedures as possible. These plans should be written, and all parties involved should be familiarized with the contents well before an actual strike materializes. An outline of the necessary concerns and considerations that should be included in such a plan appears in Figure 7–1.

To further exemplify the scope and substance of an effective strike management guide, an abbreviated sample contingency plan is provided in Figure 7–2.

No matter how carefully a strike plan is formulated at the local level, it is important to bear in mind that it will never be totally complete or comprehensive and flexible enough to anticipate every conceivable development.

TEACHER TACTICS—WHAT TO EXPECT

If you remain unconvinced of the importance of preparing a strike contingency plan, it may be helpful to remember that if the occasion arises the teachers' organization will have a well-developed action plan and will be prepared in advance to use it.

Naturally, specific strike strategies by teacher groups will vary from place to place depending on the local climate and the intensity of the dispute. Nevertheless, there are a number of tactics and techniques that are often employed before and during a teacher work stoppage. Advance knowledge of these possible actions can help school managers develop preventive measures or at least more adequate responses. The following tactics have been evident in many teacher strikes throughout the country in recent years:

- Adoption of a slow-down or work-to-rule posture prior to issuing a strike notice (some authors refer to this as a creeping strike)
- Demand for around-the-clock bargaining
- Establishment of informational picket lines
- Stepped-up media usage
- Proliferation of petitions, letters to the editor, and so on
- Establishment of crisis committees, crisis centers, truth booths, and so on
- Increasing demand for public forums and for board members to become personally involved at the table
- Charges of bad faith (unfair labor practices) on the part of the board, the superintendent, the chief negotiator for the district, and others

- Attempts to polarize the community (good guys versus bad guys)
- Emphasis on rumors, innuendoes, and half-truths
- Exploitation of students (urging pupils not to attend if schools remain open during the strike)
- Emphasis on mob psychology at rallies where strike votes are taken. These events often feature bands, slogans, banners, fight songs, fiery speakers, and open vote (no secret ballot)
- Formal picket lines (sometimes accompanied by taunts and jeers for those who cross)
- Telephone campaigning
- Boycotting of businesses owned or operated by board members
- Joint rallies with other striking locals
- Harassment
- Picketing of board members' homes
- Establishment of well-organized communication among teachers during the strike: hot lines, telephone trees, and written updates
- Community leafleting (handbills delivered to homes, shopping centers, church parking lots, and so on—Figure 7–3)
- Providing financial help for teachers during the strike (such as loans for members who participate on picket lines)
- Periodic pep rallies during the strike period
- Soliciting teachers from other districts to stage sympathy pickets

Most of the measures outlined above are generally legal and would be considered by many to be entirely reasonable.

When strikes are protracted or particularly emotion-laden, however, drastic and desperate actions sometimes occur. It is often difficult for administrators to imagine that *their* staff members would ever resort to such tactics, but as tempers and tensions mount, professionalism increasingly takes a back seat.

In difficult strike situations, it is prudent for school officials to be alert to the possibility of the following kinds of angry acts on the part of striking teachers:

- Distribution of hate literature
- Threats to board members, administrators, and family members
- Vandalism (flat tires, glue or gum in keyholes, sabotaged plumbing, and so on)
- Phone jamming
- Efforts to disrupt the school transportation system
- Physical abuse or violence on the picket lines

SOME ESSENTIAL PRECAUTIONS AND SAFEGUARDS

In addition to developing a workable contingency plan in advance, the most important considerations in managing a school strike situation are for the board and administration to maintain unity and to insist on verifiable information from all parties involved.

The six primary goals of management in a work stoppage are:

1. To press for a realistic and just settlement within a reasonable amount of time.
2. To maintain primary focus on the interests of students.
3. To retain the dignity of the district.
4. To provide for the safety of all parties and to protect the facilities and other resources of the system.
5. To preserve as much community good will and support as possible.
6. To attempt to pave the way for a rapid healing and a return to business as usual as soon as possible following the eventual settlement.

To assist administrators in all of these areas, the following precautionary measures, safeguards, and other proactive steps have proved beneficial in strike survival and successful strike management:

- Be alert to the following indicators of a pending strike: (1) protracted and heated negotiations, (2) increased militancy by staff members both inside and outside negotiation sessions (a flurry of grievances), and (3) unusual attention or involvement of state or national teacher organizations.
- Make every effort to collect all keys before the strike.
- Collect grade books, lesson plans, seating charts, and so on, before teachers leave.
- Advise teachers to take home all personal belongings for the duration of the strike.
- Teachers should be expected to turn in all school money, to leave all school-owned equipment on the premises, and to leave desks unlocked.
- Clarify the role of the building principal in advance.
- Lock up confidential files and records throughout the work stoppage.
- Develop a list of volunteers in advance.
- Hold daily briefings for all nonstriking personnel.
- In determining whether or not schools should remain open, weigh these seven considerations:
    1. Keeping the school open is one way to test the strength of the strike.

2. Most systems stay open if the striking unit is other than the teachers' organization.
3. Duration of the strike may determine the advisability of closing or remaining open.
4. If schools operate, the curriculum and program may have to be determined on a day-to-day basis.
5. Volunteers may vanish if the strike is long or the situation becomes ugly.
6. Part-time personnel not affected by the strike (such as aides) may be shifted to full-time if necessary to operate the school.
7. It is possible to keep only selected schools or parts of schools open.

- Maintain a log of all communications.
- Advise work–study students that they should continue to report to their jobs during the stoppage.
- Do not allow strikers in the building.
- Instruct principals not to converse with picket-line personnel.
- Contact other schools that have experienced strike situations for advice and counsel, but don't expect a great deal of help from the outside. (A striking district often becomes rather isolated rapidly once a strike is announced.)
- Provide for around-the-clock security and surveillance. (Private security forces may be utilized in addition to local police.)
- Lock all doors from the inside, leaving only one entrance open if possible.
- Secure power lines if possible.
- Alert insurance companies of possible public liability, property damage, and so on.
- Advise nonstriking personnel to withdraw and contact the police if they are physically prevented from crossing picket lines.
- Require reports of all incidents on the picket lines or on school premises (see sample report in Figure 7–4).
- Have legal counsel readily available at all times.
- Use court injunctions where necessary.
- Be prepared to terminate employees who participate in the strike illegally.
- If many incidents occur, consider hiring a photographer to record the activity.
- If necessary, be prepared to publish teacher salaries.
- Anticipate that your days and nights may be consumed by the media.
- Don't become unduly discouraged if the strike lasts longer than you

expected. (Short strikes sometimes encourage others, and some of the most satisfactory settlements are reached only after the strikers begin to feel the pinch of the stoppage.)

- Do your best to maintain your humanity and sense of humor throughout the difficult situation.

HOW TO PUT THE PIECES BACK TOGETHER

All of the measures identified above can assist school managers in weathering the storm of a strike situation. A more crucial challenge, however, may be posed by the task of bringing all parties involved (staff, administrators, board, and the community) back together to resume the real business of the school once a settlement has been reached.

Positive personnel management practices may help prevent strikes and may minimize upheaval and enduring harm during strikes. Additionally, however, they are essential to provide an effective means for rapidly returning to routine in the aftermath of a strike situation.

The four major tasks confronting administrators once normalcy returns after a work stoppage are:

1. To reinstate a positive, productive educational process as quickly as possible.
2. To restore internal harmony and external confidence.
3. To recharge the staff with a renewed focus and commitment to students.
4. To draw important lessons from the strike experience which can be applied to future periods of stress in staff–labor relations.

The foremost consideration in effecting the healing process is the quality of communication after a strike. Open communication is the key to restoring the maximum morale and productivity within the minimum amount of time.

The tested tips below have aided building and district administrators alike in overcoming the inevitable poststrike anticlimax syndrome and in putting the school program back on track following a work stoppage:

- Urge all parties involved to forget the past and to focus on the future.
- Keep poststrike posturing out of the classroom as much as possible.
- Refrain from attempting a reconciliation meeting.
- Minimize discussion of strike topics.
- Keep strikers and nonstriking substitutes apart for a little while.
- Avoid potentially abrasive situations that may impede the recovery process.
- Watch for overt (or sometimes subtle) recriminations.

- Expedite payrolls and makeup procedures.
- Treat all strikers and nonstrikers alike once a settlement is reached.
- Create positive outlets for pent-up emotions as soon as possible.
- Focus attention on the students.
- Resume all activity programs immediately.

By following the suggestions contained throughout this chapter, administrators at all levels can make the best of the worst personnel situation—a teacher strike.

STRIKE CONTINGENCY PLAN OUTLINE

I. Decision-making Process

A. Role of the school board

B. Role of the superintendent

C. Role of principals and other administrators

II. Communication Channels

A. Spokesperson (superintendent, board chairperson, communications co-ordinator, or other)

B. Internal
  1. Board, administration
  2. Nonstriking personnel
  3. Confidentiality
  4. Delivery system

C. External
  1. Prior approval of all written communications by superintendent or designee
  2. Community, parents
  3. Press, media releases
  4. Teacher organization, striking personnel
  5. Notification of substitutes, vendors, and so on
  6. Police, other security forces
  7. Professional organizations and agencies

III. Contingency Plans—Keeping Schools Open or Closing Schools

A. Use of substitutes and volunteers

B. Curriculum

C. Attendance

D. Transportation

E. Food service

IV. Security Measures, Emergency Plans

V. Strike Control Center (Headquarters)

VI. Status and Treatment of Nonstriking Personnel

VII. Policy on the Activity Program

A. Will contests be held during the strike?

Figure 7-1

B. Use of nonstaff coaches, supervisors, and so on

C. Number of required practice (conditioning) days after the strike and before any contests are held

D. Will games, meets, or other contests missed be forfeited, canceled, or rescheduled?

VIII. Contingency Plan for Special Education and Handicapped Students

IX. Recordkeeping

A. Inventories

B. Who works, who doesn't

C. Incident reports

X. Recovery Measures

A. Communication of settlement

B. How missed days will be made up (may be determined in the final settlement)

C. Payrolls for striking and nonstriking personnel

Figure 7–1 *(continued)*

STRIKE PLAN

Introduction

The financial crisis being experienced by the school district has brought the possibility of a strike closer. In this environment, it is essential for the administration to be prepared with contingency plans for operating the schools under strike conditions and also for closing the schools under strike conditions.

The purpose of this plan is to describe policies and procedures and to provide operating instructions to central and building administration in case of a teachers' strike.

The planning contained in this plan has attempted to anticipate conditions that might exist during a strike, but it is certain that not all eventualities have been addressed.

GENERAL INFORMATION FOR ALL ADMINISTRATORS

Basic Position of the Board

1. The district will keep the schools open and operating in the event of work stoppage as long as the health, safety, and educational welfare of students and personnel can be assured.

2. All district personnel are expected to report to their assigned duty stations and to carry out the responsibilities of their assignments to the best of their ability under the particular circumstances that exist unless notified differently by their supervisor.

3. If a strike occurs, the board will be asked to enact emergency resolutions suspending personal leave and requiring doctor's verification of sick leave for each day of sick leave.

4. In the event of a change in normal school procedures that would alter your responsibilities, you will receive instruction directly from your supervisor.

Expectations for Management Personnel

1. All cabinet personnel and classified supervisory personnel are considered management personnel.

2. All management personnel are expected to report to their assigned duty stations until and unless directed otherwise by their line superior or the superintendent of schools.

3. All management personnel will carry out the responsibilities of their assignments to the best of their ability under the particular circumstances that exist.

Figure 7–2

4. It may be necessary to redeploy management personnel to better meet building or districtwide needs. Management personnel must be prepared to assume such interim assignments, even if outside their normal field of responsibility.

Definitions of Emergency Plans

Emergency Plan 1. Schools will be open and operating. This plan will be in effect the first day of any work stoppage and all following days of school operation as long as adequate health, safety, and educational standards can be maintained in the schools with available nonstriking district employees, including administrators and certified substitute teachers.

Emergency Plan 2. Schools will be closed. If the lack of available personnel makes it impossible to maintain acceptable health, safety, and educational standards, the board may decide to implement emergency plan 2. This plan will operate as follows:

1. Schools will be closed to students and all striking groups during the work stoppage.
2. Food service personnel will not report for work during the work stoppage.
3. Transportation services will be suspended except for out-of-district special education stations and students attending out-of-district vocational-technical programs.
4. All nonstriking district groups who can perform meaningful tasks will report for work every day until further notice.
5. The principal and assistant principals will report to their buildings each day and supervise the above employees.
6. All community education programs and building use permits will be canceled.
7. All student extracurricular activities will be canceled.

The following is an alternative to the above plan:

1. Schools will be closed to students and all employees except administrators, supervisory personnel, and clerical staff.
2. All administrators, supervisory personnel, and clerical staff will report daily to their assigned duty stations and carry out their assignments, awaiting information from the superintendent.

Emergency Plan 3. If the lack of available district personnel makes it impossible to maintain acceptable health, safety, and educational standards, the board may decide to implement emergency plan 3. This plan will operate as follows:

Figure 7–2 (continued)

1. The district will seek and hire as many certified teacher substitutes as required and will initiate action to obtain necessary support services to keep schools open throughout the work stoppage.

2. On the daily school report, the principal will indicate the number of substitutes needed to reach acceptable staffing levels.

3. The principal will be notified of the names of the substitutes to be expected.

4. All other procedures from emergency plan 1 will be in effect.

Internal Communication Processes

1. Directives regarding the operating of the schools will be initiated by the superintendent, or a designee, and will be communicated through the established emergency telephone network.

2. Daily informational meetings will be held for various management groups at times and places to be announced.

External Communications

Information for the Media

1. Communications with the press will be issued only through the superintendent's or designee's office. The responsibility for statements to the press lies with the following individuals for the designated area of responsibility:

   a. General public relations statements and statements on district policy: superintendent and board chairperson

   b. Statements on conditions in the schools during the course of the work stoppage: assistant superintendent

   c. Progress of negotiations: school board spokesperson

   d. Litigation: school district counsel

2. All other management personnel should make no statement to the press at any time during the course of the work stoppage.

3. Principals will not allow media representatives to enter the buildings for information or pictures. Pictures cannot be prohibited outside the building.

Information to Parents

1. Building principals should make every effort to keep parents of their students informed regarding anticipated changes in the operation of their building. This helps to prevent misinformation and to allay fears.

Figure 7–2 *(continued)*

2. A special recorded telephone message providing current information about the status of school operation will be available to parents and the public. The telephone number to call for this message will be announced.

Payroll

The district policy for payroll is that employees will be paid only for services rendered.

During the period of the strike, all employees must sign in daily when reporting for work. Sign-in sheets will be provided for this purpose.

Personnel who report in as sick need a doctor's verification for each day claimed.

Other types of leave should be canceled. If a staff member has a true emergency (such as a death in the family), this must be authorized in advance and verified by recognizable proof (such as an article in the newspaper).

SPECIFIC INFORMATION FOR PRINCIPALS

Planning Staff Needs

Principals should plan their staffing needs during a work stoppage, estimating that half of their teachers and half of their students will be absent the first day. The principal can estimate staffing needs for the first day by using an average class student-to-teacher ratio of 32 to 1 for secondary students and 30 to 1 for elementary students. It may be necessary to increase these ratios depending on available staff resources.

Classified Staff and Volunteers

Classified staff may not be given instructional reponsibility for any class. They may be very helpful in working with small groups under a certified teacher, monitoring hallways and large group instruction (with a certificated teacher present), distributing materials, or helping with lunch service.

Volunteers also can be helpful in the above ways. It is best to limit volunteers to known individuals, preferably parents of students in that school.

Support Services

Custodians. If the custodian group is participating in the strike, it is necessary for principals to be at their buildings at the time when custodians usually unlock the doors. Principals are advised to review the opening procedure with their custodians prior to the expected work stoppage.

Food services. Students should be advised to bring their lunches and a beverage the first day of the work stoppage. For the first day of school, this information will be given to parents via the media.

Figure 7–2 *(continued)*

<u>Transportation</u>. Transportation will be provided for bussed students.

Daily Procedures

1. Each morning, every building principal will call his or her responsible administrator, reporting:

   Number of teachers present _____
   Number of teachers absent _____
   Number of classified present _____
   Number of classified absent _____
   Number of teachers needed _____
   Number of substitutes present _____
   Number of volunteers present _____
   Striking conditions _____

   This message then will be communicated to the personnel office. Names of the assigned substitutes will be phoned to the principal.

2. All schools will open and close at the usual times unless otherwise specified.

3. During a work stoppage emergency, the acceptable extraordinary class load will be as follows:

   1 to 27 the first five days
   1 to 29 the next five days
   1 to 30 thereafter for elementary and 1 to 32 for secondary

4. As mentioned above, the principal must have every employee sign in each day. Appropriate sheets will be furnished. Only the employee's signature is a valid record of his or her attendance.

5. At the end of each day of the strike, the principal will fill out a daily school report, to be submitted to his or her responsible administrator. These reports will be summarized by the assistant superintendent and submitted on the strike status summary to the superintendent.

6. Nonstriking teachers and other personnel should be encouraged to meet somewhere near the school and cross the picket line together every morning. They should select a different meeting spot every day.

7. Each principal will report attendance daily to his or her responsible administrator.

Cancellations

1. Classes involving potentially dangerous equipment or very special teaching skills should be eliminated as necessary for the duration of the work

Figure 7–2 (continued)

stoppage. Principals will be responsible for making these decisions for their buildings.

Security and Other Precautions

1. Principals should remind all teachers that class lists, seating plans, attendance cards, staff handbooks, and lesson plan books must be left in the classrooms.

2. Duplicates of the following should be prepared for substitutes: class lists and school schedules, including recesses and lunch hours, special reading or math programs, special music, art, and physical education classes.

3. All keys to exterior doors of the school should be collected by the principal the day before the expected work stoppage. This includes the custodian's keys. If the strike occurs without advance notice, the supervisor of buildings and grounds will be responsible for collecting the keys from custodial personnel.

4. All doors except the front door of the building are to be kept locked but not chained during the day. No picketers are to be permitted in the building for any reason, including use of lavatories, at any time before, during, or after school.

5. If necessary, the principal should warn picketers that picketing on school property is illegal.

6. Since security personnel will be limited, principals are advised to use any parent volunteers to patrol school grounds.

7. The principal should report any incidents of violence requiring additional protection to his or her responsible administrator.

8. If any of the following conditions exist, the principal should call his or her responsible administrator to request the closure of the school:

    a. Lack of certificated staff to maintain an acceptable pupil-to-teacher ratio
    b. Lack of water, plumbing facilities, or lighting
    c. Any unusual conditions disrupting the educational process

   In the event that the health and safety of students require an immediate closing of the building and the principal is unable to contact his or her responsible administrator, the principal shall at his or her discretion proceed to close the building.

9. If a junior high or senior high school must be closed unexpectedly during the day, the principal should call the surrounding feeder schools to inform those principals of the closure.

10. If a school must be closed early, all bussed students must be supervised until the buses arrive.

Figure 7–2 (continued)

LET'S GET BACK TO THE CLASSROOM

We know you are concerned about your child's education. Teachers also are concerned about the children and about our profession.

The teaching profession is having a difficult time attracting and keeping quality teachers because of difficult working conditions and low salaries.

Did you realize that first-year teachers with four-year college degrees earned $11,778 in our district last year? Meanwhile, their college classmates were earning an average of $18,868 in the first year on the job in other professions.

Teachers are concerned about settling this strike. You can help by calling your school board today!

Figure 7–3. Sample Leaflet

ACTIVITY/INCIDENT REPORT

Building _____ Reporter _____ Time_____

The following is an account of all unusual activities that took place at this building today. (Report details of unusual incidents such as blocking entrances, general abuse, blocking of deliveries, vandalism, damage to property, and so on.)

Time   Activity   Names

_____

_____

_____

_____

_____

_____

Figure 7–4

CHAPTER SUPPLEMENTS

The following chapter supplements are included to illustrate the principles outlined in this chapter.

Contents:

- Sample Daily School Report Form
- Model Outline for a Departmental Strike Contingency Plan
- Sample Strike Control Center Daily Log

SAMPLE DAILY SCHOOL REPORT FORM

During strike situations, many districts have found it helpful to require daily reports from each school or building in order to monitor events and develop a profile of strike activity as the basis for day-to-day decision making. This sample form provides a simple reporting format for this purpose.

Date _____   Time _____

School _____

Person reporting _____ Position _____

1. Principal present   Yes _____ No _____
2. Number of assistant principals   Present _____ Absent _____
3. Number of your regular faculty
   present   _____
4. Number of your regular faculty
   absent   _____
5. Number of other faculty present   _____
6. Number of reserve teachers
   present   _____
7. Number of reserve teachers
   needed   _____
8. Number of teacher aides present   _____
9. Head custodian present   Yes _____ No _____
10. Number of other custodians   Present _____ Absent _____
11. Building operation:

   Light   Adequate _____ Inadequate _____
   Heat   Adequate _____ Inadequate _____
   Water   Adequate _____ Inadequate _____

12. School secretary present   Yes _____ No _____
13. Number of other clerical staff   Present _____ Absent _____
14. Number of food service staff   Present _____ Absent _____
15. Food available   Yes _____ No _____
16. Faculty pickets   Yes _____ No _____ # _____
17. Student pickets   Yes _____ No _____ # _____
18. Approximate number of students   Present _____ Absent _____
19. If your school receives bus students,
    did buses arrive?   Yes _____ No _____
20. School program status   Normal _____ Reduced _____
                                         Limited _____ Suspended _____

MODEL OUTLINE
FOR A DEPARTMENTAL
STRIKE CONTINGENCY PLAN

Certain departments within the school—vocational education, special education, community education, and so on—are well advised to develop their own strike contingency plans to meet the particular needs of their area of operation. This model outline earmarks essential components of such a plan.

Department Strike Contingency Plan

Department _____

1. <u>Supervisory employees</u>   Total personnel _____

   Personnel required for priority service _____

   Personnel available for personnel pool _____

2. <u>Priority 1 services</u> (services that must not be interrupted during the first hour of the strike)

   List with person assigned to each duty:

3. <u>Priority 2 services</u> (services that can go unattended for up to one week during a strike)

   List with person assigned to each duty:

4. <u>Priority 3 services</u> (services that can go unattended for up to 30 days after a strike is initiated)

5. <u>Priority 4 services</u> (services that can go unattended for longer than 30 days after the initiation of a strike)

SAMPLE STRIKE CONTROL CENTER DAILY LOG

Telephone _____   Date _____

Answer: "Hello, identify your school and yourself please."

DUTY (initial in)	CALL TIME	SCHOOL	CALLER	COMMENTS

8

Some Final Tips

The intent of this handbook has been to define in clearcut terms some new marching orders for today's school leaders in the area of effective personnel management. The practices described throughout are designed to go beyond time-worn, simplistic recipes for administration and supervision and to reveal alternatives that can be used to improve all schools in the context of modern living, learning, and labor relationships.

In order to strengthen the value of the guide as a straightforward self-help manual for school leaders, this final chapter offers additional aids in modernizing personnel management under current conditions and ties all of the elements outlined earlier into a meaningful, overall approach that is working in many school settings today and will become standard operating procedures tomorrow.

HOW TO USE THE ENCOURAGING PROCESS TO IMPROVE PRODUCTIVITY

The style of management advocated throughout this text is based on the realization that changing times, shifting values, and an emerging new work force require personnel practices that emphasize liberation (not limitation) and encouragement (rather than oppression) of employees at all levels. The essence of such an approach is a dramatic shift from supervisory control derived from power, intimidation, and autocracy, to a new form of leadership rooted in commitment to the concept of encouragement as a means of fostering productive working relationships and attaining necessary organizational outcomes.

At the heart of an encouraging approach to providing leadership for school personnel is a willingness to practice what some successful administrators label as Management by Expectancy. Countless studies have demonstrated that teacher expectations dictate achievement by students. What teachers expect, they usually receive in terms of pupil performance. It is surprising that school leaders have been slow to realize that the same principles apply in managing professional staffs and other adult employees.

In the modern context of personnel management wherein power has been redistributed through negotiated agreements and prescribed fair labor relations rules, effective leadership must evolve from motivation rather than mandates. The most successful route to productivity and performance by school staffs is through an unflinching emphasis on positive expectation and encouragement by management, coupled with a clearcut awareness on the part of staff members of administration's belief in their potential and readiness to apply resources to help them achieve their full promise and level of effectiveness.

The modern view of personnel administration built on management by expectancy and a proactive process of encouragement stems from these ten premises for promoting productivity:

1. Inherent distrust and adversarial relationships are not inescapable conditions of working in public school systems.

2. Becoming an encourager can help the administrator as much as or more than his or her subordinates.

3. Every employee has untapped potential.

4. There is just reason for an optimistic view of the possibilities for change within any staff.

5. Encouraging leaders expect the best and often get it.

6. If employees are induced to expect better performance from themselves, they can and will achieve.

7. Any staff member (teacher or other employee) can move from the paralyzing perception of "I can't" to the openness of "I can try."

8. The aggregate strength within any organization emerges from a sense of interconnectedness (a "we" view of mutual support).

9. The goal of an encouraging process of personnel management is development of a total staff comprised of persons who take responsibility, see options, are risk takers, avoid undue compliance, are in touch with their own priorities, and can agree to disagree.

10. Improvement in performance is usually a gradual process of making a little positive change each day.

In order to understand more fully the factors that make up management by expectancy and the encouraging process, the diagram in Figure 8–1 points up

POSITIVE AND NEGATIVE RESPONSES

**Elements that
encourage success**

High expectations

Demonstrations of faith

Efforts to build self-respect and
   esteem

Focus on existing strengths

Maintaining a sense of humor
   and universal human frailty

Recognition of effort and
   progress

Capitalizing on staff interests

Responsiveness to needs

Genuine willingness in helping
   coworkers grow and achieve

**Elements that
discourage success**

Lack of support

Threats and intimidation

Criticism

Judgmental behavior

Pessimistic view of success

Insensitivity

Lecturing

Squelching initiative and
   suggestions for improvement

A know-it-all attitude

Moralizing

Withholding resources

Reproof through silence

Figure 8–1

common elements that encourage and discourage employee success and productive performances.

SURE-FIRE STEPS FOR OPENING UP THE SYSTEM

One fundamental facet of promoting positive personnel management through the expectancy and encouraging process is the exercise of leadership in opening up the system (at the building or district level) to meaningful staff input and involvement. This section suggests a menu of measures for enhancing such participatory decision making and problem solving.

The straightforward motto of the widely known Common Cause consumer and citizen organization led by John Gardner is simply the acronym OUTS standing for an admonition to "Open Up The System."

The same slogan might well be adopted as the watchword for successful personnel management in schools. One of the principles for practicing an expectancy-based approach to supervision is to expand opportunity for staff contribution to improving productivity, morale, and overall effectiveness. Below are 19 school-tested steps for promoting internal communication, cooperation, and collaboration which have helped open up the system in a variety of school environments:

1. Adopt an up-front posture in communicating problems as well as sharing successes with the entire staff.

2. Provide opportunities for employees at all levels to periodically critique the performance of the principal and other supervisors (such as an annual Administrator's Report Card).

3. Sample staff opinion on all important issues and matters affecting the entire school.

4. Arrange faculty retreats for purposes of brainstorming and planning.

5. Establish routine channels of communication with key opinion leaders within all categories of employees.

6. Hold regular meetings of department heads, grade-level chairpersons, and program leaders as a forum for determining school policy and direction.

7. Encourage staff members to attend school board meetings to remain abreast of districtwide developments.

8. Include a public concerns portion on all school board agendas to enable staff members as well as members of the community to express views, air concerns, and ask questions.

9. Permit staff to plan faculty meeting agendas whenever possible.

10. Issue weekly bulletins to apprise staff of current schoolwide activities and upcoming events.

11. Post agendas of all school board, departmental, and faculty meetings well in advance.

12. Permit staff members to participate in the recruitment, selection, and hiring of new personnel, including department heads, supervisors, and even the principal (see the sample participation letter in Figure 8–2).

13. Encourage all staff members to become involved in networking as a source of support and idea exchange.

14. Maximize the use of internal written organs of communication (weekly bulletings, staff letters, know-your-school reports, monthly miscellany updates, and so on). Include an open section for staff comments in all publications.

15. Adopt an official policy statement pertaining to staff participation (see sample policy in Figure 8–3).

16. Explore applications of the Japanese concept of quality circles to the educational scene. (A quality circle is a small group of people, usually eight to fifteen, from the same work area, who meet regularly to identify, analyze, and develop solutions to work-related problems. Such programs are based on the concept that the person who knows the most about an individual job is the one who does it on a daily basis.)

17. Involve staff in the selection of all instructional materials and supplies (including computer courseware and other media materials).

18. Promote staff participation in special-interest and advisory groups within the district (such as the Council for Gifted and Talented).

19. Explore the possibility of decentralizing power and decision making through a system of school-site (school-based) management (see the characteristics of a school-site management program in Figure 8–4).

MORE WAYS TO WORK WITH THE NEW EDUCATIONAL WORK FORCE

In addition to the strategies and techniques contained throughout this text and the special helps for opening up the system described above, some further pointers have been successful in several settings for making school personnel practices more relevant to today's needs.

As work roles are changing in schools everywhere, management is increasingly being required to adopt a more responsive leadership style. The traditional play-it-safe management model, with its built-in suspicion and adversarial relationships, is no longer applicable to the modern school. With swift and permeating shifts in rules, definitions, norms, and administrative patterns, school leaders at all levels are discovering some new principles of positive personnel management. At the core of the new concept of school leadership are the beliefs that all employees must find some inner joy in the work place and that human interaction is ultimately the best teacher for everyone involved.

Central School
100 Main Street
Anywhere, U.S.A.

To: Parents and Staff of the Anywhere community

The search for a principal for Central School proceeds. The school board and the PSSA invites you to become involved in this interesting adventure. The finalists for the position are:

_____

_____

_____

_____

Final interviews are scheduled for May 13, 14, 15, and 20. During each evening (7:30 P.M.), the principal candidates will be at the school to meet community and staff members.

As part of each evening's session, we have asked each candidate to say a few things about himself or herself in order to give those present a better feeling for them as people as well as principals. We will also provide time for a few questions from the floor, although it is not the intent to turn this into a mass interview. The rest of the evening will allow for informal conversation and a chance for those present to introduce themselves to the principal candidates.

After you have had a chance to meet the candidates, if any of you wish to forward comments for our consideration in making the final selection, they should be sent in writing to the superintendent's office no later than May 21. We are not looking for votes or rankings, but any comments you send will be considered in making the final selection. Telephone comments cannot be accepted and are therefore discouraged.

Sincerely,

Figure 8–2

STAFF INVOLVEMENT IN DECISION MAKING

It shall be the policy of the board to encourage employee participation in decision making for the school district. The superintendent is authorized to establish such committees as necessary to recommend policies and rules for the proper functioning of the district.

All professional personnel shall be encouraged to assist in the formulation of recommended educational policy for the district through their representatives on the Superintendent's Advisory Council.

In the development of rules, regulations, and arrangements for the operation of the school system, the superintendent shall include at the planning stage whenever feasible those employees who will be affected by such provisions.

The superintendent shall evolve with employees channels for the ready intercommunication of ideas and feelings regarding the operation of the schools. The superintendent shall weigh with care the counsel given by employees, especially that given by groups designated to represent large segments of the staff, and shall inform the board of all such counsel in presenting reports of administrative action and in presenting recommendations for board action.

Figure 8–3

CHARACTERISTICS OF A SCHOOL-SITE MANAGEMENT PROGRAM

- Movement of many management prerogatives to the local school site
- Delegation of authority, control, and power from the school board and central administration to building-level units
- Shared decision making by the teachers, principal, parents, and community members at the building level
- Increased participation and influence by parents
- Formation of a parent–citizen council to work with staff and students on school-based problems and concerns
- Building-level autonomy over school budgeting, staffing patterns, program design, staff development, and so on.

Figure 8–4

Effective managers are rapidly realizing that for leadership to be successful employees must feel that administration understands the group, seeks help where needed, and evaluates alternative courses of action carefully. When these conditions exist, even the new breed of employee can accept mistakes by management based on their belief that the process of decision making has included consideration for all. Staff members at all levels continue to respond to tough, direct leadership as long as it is based on a track record of fair play.

With this view of positive personnel management in mind, the practical, supplemental suggestions that follow can aid any administrator in providing more effective leadership for the entire school staff:

- Concentrate on climate setting. The goal should be an environment in which all employees can grow toward success with the realization that all growth entails some pain as well as rewards.

- Adopt the principle of the Plural Executive by including appropriate staff members in the inner circle of decision making whenever possible. Administrative survival necessitates delegation, and effective team building requires active, responsible, and meaningful involvement by many people.

- Explore ways to share and exchange staff members with local business and industry.

- Encourage active involvement and participation by all employees in professional organizations. (Encouraging staff participation in union organizations is usually not a role management chooses to play or really needs to play.)

- Permit employee input in the development of all job descriptions, even their own.

- Hold regular Monday morning staff meetings to share all of the good things that happened the previous week. (Some administrators have found this to be a valuable device for setting a positive tone in the school, jacking up morale, and dispelling infectious staff cynicism or pessimism.)

- Form a principal's cabinet similar to the superintendent's cabinet found in many school districts.

- Encourage and provide funds for staff attendance at conferences and conventions where appropriate.

- Promote interstaff, interlevel support (see sample memo in Figure 8–5).

- Recognize contributions to the community by staff members.

- Promote and encourage media attention to what teachers are doing in the classroom. (Some districts invite popular TV reporters to teach a day or portion of a day during American Education Week and to air their experiences.)

TO: Elementary Principals and Teachers

FROM: Junior High Eighth Grade Global Geography Teachers

CONGRATULATIONS!!!   THANKS!!!   KEEP UP THE GOOD WORK!!!

You're doing a terrific job in teaching reading to kids before their Junior High days.

Last year and this year we tested all eighth grade students in our geography classes with the Gates–MacGinitie Reading Survey. The results both years were surprisingly identical:

	Average Grade Level Class of '88	Average Grade Level Class of '89
Vocabulary	9.5	9.5
Comprehension	9.1	9.1

Plainly stated, the eighth grade students are reading from 1 to 1½ grade levels above average. We feel we are the direct beneficiaries of the excellent teaching going on in the elementary grades.

Again, CONGRATULATIONS!!!   THANKS!!!   KEEP 'EM COMING!!!

Figure 8–5

- Free up people to develop curriculum materials and educational computer courseware for publication, with royalties coming to the district. (Sometimes arrangements can be made to provide employees as experts on loan to publishers or computer software firms for this purpose.)
- Provide released time for staff participation on districtwide committees (Staff Development Committee, Textbook Selection Committees, and so on).
- Seek ways to "re-pot" personnel every five years. (Although most employees resist change or transfer, once it is accomplished positive growth usually occurs.)
- Reward excellence and productivity in every way possible.

Taken separately, each of the practices and procedures delineated above and in preceding chapters represents individual steps toward improved personnel management by school administrators. Collectively, however, they comprise a comprehensive total program of fluid, flexible leadership capable of satisfying the demands of changing organizational structures and relationships.

USING THE CONCEPT OF "HUMANAGEMENT" AS A TOOL FOR POSITIVE PERSONNEL MANAGEMENT

The model of supervisory leadership presented in this text represents a radical departure from traditional caretaker management and offers a bold, fresh approach to maximizing productivity in schools. Some authors have defined this new style of action as the process of "humanagement." The primary tenets of this new view of humanistic personnel management are the following:

- School leaders are both the shapers and the shakers of the work environment and thus are ultimately responsible for the overall effectiveness of the staff and the organization as a whole.
- Successful leadership in today's school requires working with people in ways that blur historic distinctions in power, position, and importance among levels of personnel.
- Humanizing personnel management practices is not a retreat toward ineffectual leadership but rather an advance based on people interacting to develop improved relationships and more productive outcomes.
- Productivity results from promoting the worth of every employee and the work each does.
- Authentic participatory decision making can help meet the needs of both the individual employee and the organization simultaneously.
- Professionals organized to pursue mutual growth and success are more effective than employees rooted in routine.

- The essence of effective leadership and positive working relationships is trust, as diagramed below:

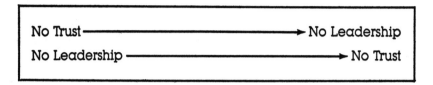

- A working climate designed to promote growth features structured caring, not coddling.

The contrasts between business-as-usual personnel practices of the past and the emerging concept of management based on expectancy and encouragement are sharply illustrated by the management models that appear in Figure 8–6.

One further perspective on the view of positive personnel management advocated throughout this guide is provided in the list of pros and cons outlined in Figure 8–7.

The positive handling of personnel serves increasingly as the critical determiner of the success or failure of educational leaders. The three Rs of modern administrative leadership are clearly becoming responsiveness, respect, and responsibility.

In the pressurized atmosphere of a transformative educational context, negativism can be contagious. The challenge to administrators and supervisors in this super-charged atmosphere of change is to maximize positive aspects of people and programs, to build on existing strengths, and to promote optimal use of all human resources in the school.

Since people represent the school's greatest resource and the largest investment (70 to 80 percent of most school budgets), effective people management marks the successful leader in today's school. In fact, if administrators can solve the human equation in the school and can successfully manage interpersonal relationships, other administrative functions, such as caring for buses, buildings, and budgets, will become relatively easy matters to handle.

The philosophical framework and the extensive array of action steps provided throughout this handbook can serve as a guide for employing positive personnel management to make any school a better, more productive place to work and learn.

Traditional Management Model

- Order
- Sanctions
- Rigid
- Punitive
- Impersonal
- Autocratic
- Compliance

Humanistic Management Model

- Respect
- Success-oriented
- Open
- Interactive
- Fair
- Self-discipline

Figure 8–6

PROS AND CONS OF
HUMANISTIC MANAGEMENT
("HUMANAGEMENT")

Pros
- Increased trust
- Enhanced communication
- Clearer concept of goals
- Improved performance and productivity
- Better planning
- More job satisfaction
- Reduced frustration
- Heightened accountability
- Improved chance for change

Cons
- Time-consuming
- Perceived ambuiguity
- Discomfort with lack of structure
- Greater risk

Figure 8–7

CHAPTER SUPPLEMENTS

The following chapter supplement is included to illustrate the principles outlined in this chapter.

Content:

- Selected Bibliography on Positive Personnel Management for Educators

SELECTED BIBLIOGRAPHY ON
POSITIVE PERSONNEL MANAGEMENT
FOR EDUCATORS

Bittel, Lester R. What Every Supervisor Should Know. New York: McGraw-Hill Book Company, 1980.

Blake, Robert R., and June S. Mouton. Productivity: The Human Side. New York: American Management Association, 1981.

Chernow, Fred, and Carol Chernow. School Administrator's Guide to Managing People. West Nyack, N.Y.: Parker Publishing Company, 1976.

Drucker, Peter F., The Effective Executive. New York: Harper and Row, 1966.

Gregoric, Anthony F. An Adult's Guide to Style. Maynard, Mass.: Gabriel Systems, Inc., 1982.

Heller, Robert. The Great Executive Dream. New York: Delacorte Press, 1972.

Judson, Arnold S. A Manager's Guide to Making Changes. New York: John Wiley & Sons, Inc., 1966.

Nierachberg, Gerald I. The Art of Negotiating. New York: Simon and Schuster, 1968.

Ouchi, William, Theory Z. Reading, Mass.: Addison-Wesley Publishing Company, 1981.

Ramsey, Robert D. Educator's Discipline Handbook. West Nyack, N.Y.: Parker Publishing Company, Inc., 1981.

Stanton, Erwin R. Reality-Centered People Management: Key to Improved Productivity. New York: American Management Association, 1982.

Walling, Donovan R. Complete Book of School Public Relations: An Administrator's Manual and Guide. Englewood Cliffs, N.J.: Prentice-Hall, Inc., 1982.

Index

All page numbers in italics indicate an illustrative form(s).